School Teachers' Pay and Conditions Document 2008 And Guidance on School Teachers' Pay and Conditions

TSO
information & publishing solutions

Published by TSO (The Stationery Office) and available from:

Online
www.tsoshop.co.uk

Mail, Telephone, Fax and E-mail
TSO
PO Box 29, Norwich, NR3 1GN
Telephone orders/General enquiries: 0870 600 5522
Fax orders: 0870 600 5533
E-mail: customer.services@tso.co.uk
Textphone 0870 240 3701

TSO Shops
16 Arthur Street, Belfast BT1 4GD
028 9023 8451 Fax 028 9023 5401
71 Lothian Road, Edinburgh EH3 9AZ
0870 606 5566 Fax 0870 606 5588

TSO@Blackwell and other Accredited Agents

Department for Children, Schools and Families
Sanctuary Buildings
Great Smith Street
London SW1P 3BT

Tel: 0870 011 2345

First Published 2008
978-0-11-271198-8

Printed by The Stationery Office Limited under the authority and superintendence of the Controller of Her Majesty's Stationery Office and the Queen's Printer of Acts of Parliament.

Text is printed on 100% recycled material
Cover is printed on 75% recycled material

N5871769 C400 9/08

CONTENTS

SECTION 1 – Introductory

Note: This introductory section does not form part of either the statute (the School Teachers' Pay and Conditions Document in Section 2 of this publication) or the statutory guidance (Sections 3 and 4 of this publication).

Introduction

1. The Education Act 2002 gives the Secretary of State power to issue guidance on pay and conditions matters, to which those concerned must have regard.

2. Since 2003 this publication has brought together the two key parts of the framework for the England and Wales pay arrangements – the School Teachers' Pay and Conditions Document ('the Document') and the statutory guidance. These may also be found at www.teachernet.gov.uk/pay. The Document (Section 2 – the statute) and the guidance (Sections 3 and 4 – the statutory guidance) need to be read together to provide a complete picture of pay and conditions arrangements for teachers in England and Wales.

3. The statutory requirements for teachers' pay and conditions for maintained schools in England and Wales are set out in the Document, and schools and local authorities (LAs) must abide by these. LAs and governing bodies are required to have regard to the statutory guidance, and in respect of guidance on procedural matters a court or tribunal may take any failure to do so into account in any proceedings. Broadly speaking, this means that any party not following this guidance would need to have good reason not to do so and would need to be able to justify any departure from it.

4. There have been a number of changes to the Document since the 2007 version. Details are set out in paragraph 9 below.

5. LAs and schools can find additional informative material on pay matters on Teachernet, at www.teachernet.gov.uk/pay. This material includes explanatory notes on the Document, a model pay policy and model pay statements, and guidance on pay safeguarding, with examples. Hard copies of this material can be sent on request; please call 0870 0012345 or email info@dcsf.gsi.gov.uk. Other material is available at http://www.teachernet.gov.uk/management/payandperformance/threshold/(threshold), http://www.teachernet.gov.uk/management/payandperformance/pay/excellent teacher scheme/ (Excellent Teachers), www.teachernet.gov.uk/professionaldevelopment/ast (Advanced Skills Teachers) and http://www.dcsf.gov.uk/citychallenge/london.shtml (Chartered London Teachers). For general pay queries please call 0870 0012345 or email info@dcsf.gsi.gov.uk.

6. The changes to the Document which have been made since 2007 result from School Teachers' Review Body (STRB) recommendations in January 2008 and April 2008, and agreements and discussions with the Rewards and Incentives Group[1] - the national pay partners group set up following the January 2004 Agreement. The group has agreed the guidance on general pay issues in Section 3 and is continuing to meet with the aim of agreeing further matters relating to teachers' pay and conditions.

7. In addition, the Document (Section 2) and statutory guidance (Sections 3 and 4) were consulted on with all key stakeholders as part of the normal statutory consultation process.

8. It should be noted that the three year safeguarding provisions attached to certain discontinued allowances will end on 31 December 2008. The allowances in question were: Management Allowance, Social Priority Allowance, and Inner London Area supplement.

Summary of changes to pay and conditions since 2007

9. The main changes to the Document since 2007 are as follows (paragraph references are to paragraphs in the Document):

- pay scales bringing in a 2.45% pay award from 1 September 2008 have been incorporated (paragraphs 6.4, 17.3, 19.2, 29.1 and 37.3);

- an increase of 2.45% in the value of the TLR1 and TLR2 ranges (paragraph 22.2) from 1 September 2008; a requirement to increase all TLRs in payment by 2.45% from 1 September 2008 (paragraph 23); and provision to increase by 2.45% from 1 September 2008 all TLRs which are in the staffing structure but which have not yet been awarded (paragraph 24);

- an increase of 2.45% in the value of SEN allowances (paragraph 26.1);

- additional increases for some main and upper pay scale teachers in inner and outer London;

1 Members of RIG are ASCL, ATL, DCSF, NAHT, NASUWT, NEOST, and Voice.

- new arrangements for excellent teachers' pay, following a STRB recommendation in their 15th report (2005). From 1 September 2008, excellent teachers will be paid on a spot salary within a range (paragraph 35);

- the unqualified teachers' pay scale has been shortened from 10 points to six, to meet concerns on gender and age discrimination. The criteria for the award of the unqualified teachers' allowance are also being tightened up (paragraph 37);

- a standardisation of the method of calculating pay (paragraph 49) and working time (paragraph 77) for part-time teachers has been introduced to bring about consistency of practice.

- Annex 4 signals future changes that will have effect from September 2009.

Amendments to section 3 and section 4 guidance

10. A number of amendments, updates and clarifications have been made to the statutory pay guidance in section 3, in line with the 2008 changes to the Document and comments made in the statutory consultation process.

11. In the statutory guidance on changes to the Document resulting from the National Agreement, in section 4, no changes were made this year.

Professional Standards for Teachers in England from September 2007[2]

Introduction

Bringing coherence to the professional and occupational standards for the whole school workforce

1. The framework of professional standards for teachers[3] will form part of a wider framework of standards for the whole school workforce. This includes the Training and Development Agency for Schools' (TDA) review of the occupational standards for teaching/classroom assistants and the professional standards for higher level teaching assistants in consultation with social partners and other key stakeholders and a review of leadership standards informed by the independent review of the roles and responsibilities of head teachers and the leadership group.

What these standards cover

2. The framework of professional standards for teachers defines the characteristics of teachers at each career stage. Specifically it provides professional standards for:

- the award of Qualified Teacher Status (QTS) **(Q)**
- teachers on the main scale (Core) **(C)**
- teachers on the upper pay scale (Post-Threshold Teachers) **(P)**
- Excellent Teachers **(E)**
- Advanced Skills Teachers (ASTs) **(A)**

3. Professional standards are statements of a teacher's professional attributes, professional knowledge and understanding, and professional skills. They provide clarity of the expectations at each career stage. The standards are not to be confused with and do not replace the professional duties contained in this Document, which set out the roles and responsibilities of teachers.

2 The framework as a whole applies in England only. The standards for Post-Threshold Teachers, Excellent Teachers and ASTs are pay standards (as set out in Annex 1 of the Document in Section 2) and apply in England and Wales.

3 The framework can be found at www.tda.gov.uk/standards.

4. The framework of standards below is arranged in three interrelated sections covering:

a. professional attributes
b. professional knowledge and understanding
c. professional skills

How the standards will be used

5. The standards provide the framework for a teacher's career and clarify what progression looks like. As now, to access each career stage a teacher will need to demonstrate that he/she has met the relevant standards. The process for this varies depending on the standard concerned. Teachers seeking Excellent Teacher or AST status need to apply and be assessed through an external assessment process. Teachers seeking to cross the threshold are assessed by their head teacher. The standards for Post-Threshold Teachers, Excellent Teachers and ASTs are pay standards and teachers who are assessed as meeting them also access the relevant pay scale.

6. The standards clarify the professional characteristics that a teacher should be expected to maintain and to build on at their current career stage. After the induction year, therefore, teachers would be expected to continue to meet the core standards and to broaden and deepen their professional attributes, knowledge, understanding and skills within that context. This principle applies at all subsequent career stages. So, for example, teachers who have gone through the threshold would be expected to meet the core and post-threshold standards and to broaden and deepen their professional attributes, knowledge, understanding and skills in that context. There are no new criteria for pay progression for teachers paid on the upper pay scale in this Document.

7. The standards will support teachers in identifying their professional development needs. Where teachers wish to progress to the next career stage, the next level of the framework provides a reference point for all teachers when considering future development. Whilst not all teachers will necessarily want to move to the next career stage, the standards will also support teachers in identifying ways to broaden and deepen their expertise within their current career stages.

8. All teachers should have a professional responsibility to be engaged in effective, sustained and relevant professional development throughout their careers and all teachers should have a contractual entitlement to effective, sustained and relevant professional development throughout their careers. There should be a continuum of expectations about the level of engagement in professional development that provides clarity and appropriate differentiation for each career stage. The expectations about the contribution teachers make to the development of others should take account of their levels of skills, expertise and experience, their role within the school, and reflect their use of up-to-date subject knowledge and pedagogy.[4]

9. In all these cases, performance management is the key process. Performance management provides the context for regular discussions about teachers' career aspirations and their future development, within or beyond their current career stage. The framework of professional standards will provide a backdrop to discussions about how a teacher's performance should be viewed in relation to their current career stage and the career stage they are approaching. The relevant standards should be looked at as a whole in order to help teachers identify areas of strength and areas for further professional development. For example, a teacher who aspires to become an AST will need to reflect on and discuss how they might plan their future development so they can work towards becoming an AST, and performance management would provide evidence for the teacher's future application.

10. All qualified teachers in maintained schools and non-maintained special schools are required to be registered with the GTCE. To maintain registration they must uphold the GTCE's Code of Conduct and Practice for Registered Teachers.

11. The recommendation for the award of qualified teacher status and registration with the GTCE is made by an accredited Initial Teacher Training (ITT) provider following an assessment which shows that all of the QTS standards have been met. The newly qualified teacher (NQT) may then begin the induction period. NQTs will not be required to meet fully the core standards until the end of their induction period. The core standards underpin all the subsequent standards and, where there is no progression at subsequent career

4 Extract from the Rewards and Incentives Group (RIG) evidence (Section 9 'The New Teacher Professionalism') to the STRB on 25 May 2005.

stages, are valid at all points of teachers' careers within both their immediate workplace and the wider professional context in which they work. Each set of standards builds on the previous set, so that a teacher being considered for the threshold would need to satisfy the post-threshold standards (**P**) and meet the core standards (**C**); a teacher aspiring to become an Excellent Teacher would need to satisfy the standards that are specific to that status (**E**) and meet the preceding standards (**C** and **P**); and a teacher aspiring to become an AST would need to satisfy the standards that are specific to that status (**A**) as well as meet the preceding standards (**C**, **P** and **E**) – although they can apply for an AST post before going through the threshold. In practice, the standards relating to the excellence of their own teaching are common to ASTs and Excellent Teachers, the three additional AST standards are focused on their ability to carry out their work with other schools and on their leadership role.

12. The framework of standards is progressive, reflecting the progression expected of teachers as their professional attributes, knowledge and understanding and skills develop and they demonstrate increasing effectiveness in their roles. Post-threshold Teachers are able to act as role models for teaching and learning, make a distinctive contribution to raising standards across the school, continue to develop their expertise post-threshold and provide regular coaching and mentoring to less experienced teachers. Excellent Teachers provide an exemplary model to others through their professional expertise, have a leading role in raising standards by supporting improvements in teaching practice and support and help their colleagues to improve their effectiveness and to address their development needs through highly effective coaching and mentoring. ASTs provide models of excellent and innovative teaching and use their skills to enhance teaching and learning by undertaking and leading school improvement activities and continuing professional development (CPD) for other teachers. They carry out developmental work across a range of workplaces and draw on the experience they gain elsewhere to improve practice in their own and other schools.

13. All the standards are underpinned by the five key outcomes for children and young people identified in *Every Child Matters* and the six areas of the *Common core of skills and knowledge for the children's workforce*. The work of practising teachers should be informed by an awareness, appropriate to their level of experience and responsibility, of legislation concerning the development and

well-being of children and young people expressed in the Children Act 2004, the Disability Discrimination Acts 1995 and 2005 and relevant associated guidance, the special educational needs provisions in the Education Act 1996 and the associated *Special Educational Needs: Code of Practice* (DfES 2001), the Race Relations Act 1976 as amended by the Race Relations (Amendment) Act 2000, and the guidance *Safeguarding children in education* (DfES 2004).

14. The professional standards must operate in the context of teachers' legal rights and contractual entitlements.

15. Nothing in the professional standards militates against teachers taking lawful industrial action.

Note on the terminology used in the standards

- The term 'learners' is used instead of 'children and young people' when learning per se is the main focus of the standard. It refers to all children and young people including those with particular needs, for example, those with special educational needs, looked after children, those for whom English is an additional language, those who are not reaching their potential or those who are gifted and talented.

- The term 'colleagues' is used for all those professionals with whom a teacher might work. It encompasses teaching colleagues, the wider workforce within an educational establishment, and also those from outside with whom teachers may be expected to have professional working relationships, for example early years and health professionals and colleagues working in children's services.

- The term 'classroom' is used to encompass all the settings within and beyond the workplace where teaching and learning take place.

- The term 'workplace' refers to the range of educational establishments, contexts and settings (both in and outside the classroom) where teaching takes place.

- The term 'subjects/curriculum areas' is used to cover all forms of organised learning experienced across the curriculum. For example, areas of learning in the foundation stage, broad areas of curricular experience and learning through play in the early years, thematically structured work in the primary phase, single subjects, vocational subjects and cross-curricular work in the 14–19 phase.

- The terms 'lessons' or 'sequences of lessons' are used to cover teaching and learning activities wherever they take place, whatever their nature and length, and however they might be organised, and are applicable to all educational phases and contexts.

- Where the phrase 'parents and carers' is used, it is understood that the term 'parents' includes both mothers and fathers.

- The term 'well-being' refers to the rights of children and young people (as set out, and consulted upon in the Every Child Matters Green Paper and subsequently set out in the Children Act 2004), in relation to:

  - physical and mental health and emotional well-being
  - protection from harm and neglect
  - education, training and recreation
  - the contribution made by them to society
  - social and economic well-being

- The term 'personalised learning' means maintaining a focus on individual progress, in order to maximise all learners' capacity to learn, achieve and participate. This means supporting and challenging each learner to achieve national standards and gain the skills they need to thrive and succeed throughout their lives. 'Personalising learning' is not about individual lesson plans or individualisation (where learners are taught separately or largely through a one-to-one approach).

Standards for Teachers in Wales

It should be noted that the framework for professional standards outlined in the above box is not applicable to teachers in Wales.

However, the statutory pay standards that form part of the framework for post-threshold, excellent and Advanced Skills Teachers set out in annex 1 of the Document (section 2) are applicable to teachers in both England and Wales – see the statutory pay guidance (section 3) for further guidance.

This means that the position for teachers in Wales is:

- The setting of Qualified Teacher Status (QTS) standards is the responsibility of the Welsh Assembly Government. The QTS standards are set out in legislation which can be accessed at: http://new.wales.gov.uk/legislation/legislationinforce/210923/EducaWales1/2006/QTSStandards2006e?lang=en

- The setting of the End of Induction Standard for Newly Qualified Teachers is also the responsibility of the Welsh Assembly Government. The standard and relevant guidance (circular 21/2006) can be accessed at: www.opsi.gov.uk/legislation/wales/wsi2005/20051818e.htm

- Post-threshold teachers, excellent teachers and Advanced Skills teachers - pay standards as contained within the Schools Teachers' Pay and Conditions Document 2008;

- The Welsh Assembly Government has also made the National Professional Qualification for Headship (NPQH) mandatory for all headteachers taking up their first substantive head teacher post from September 2005. A copy of the regulations can be accessed at: http://www.wales-legislation.hmso.gov.uk/legislation/wales/w-stat.htm

SECTION 2 – School Teachers' Pay and Conditions Document 2008

This Document contains provisions relating to the statutory conditions of employment of school teachers in England and Wales and has been prepared by the Secretary of State for Children, Schools and Families in anticipation of an order being made by him under section 122 of the Education Act 2002 ("the Act")(1). That Order refers to this Document and directs that its provisions have effect in accordance with it pursuant to section 124(3) of the Act. The anticipated order will be the Education (School Teachers' Pay and Conditions) Order 2008 ("the Order").

This Document relates to teachers employed by a local education authority or by the governing body of a foundation, voluntary aided or foundation special school (other than a school to which an order made under section 128(2) of the Act applies) in the provision of primary or secondary education (otherwise than in an establishment maintained by a local authority in the exercise of a social services function).

When the Order comes into force, this Document will from 1st September 2008 replace the 2007 Document given effect by the Education (School Teachers' Pay and Conditions) Order 2007(2).

Department for Children, Schools and Families
Sanctuary Buildings
Great Smith Street
London SW1P 3BT

Tel: 0870 0012345

(1) 2002 c.32.
(2) S.I. 2007/2282.

Contents

SECTION 2

Allowances for classroom teachers

Advanced skills teachers

Assessment against the advanced skills teacher standards and the excellent teacher standards

Excellent teachers and chartered London teachers

PART 5 – Unqualified Teachers

PART 6 – Additional Allowances

PART 7 – Supplementary

CONDITIONS OF EMPLOYMENT

PART 8 – General

PART 9 – Conditions of Employment of Head Teachers

SECTION 2

PART 10 – Conditions of Employment of Deputy Head Teachers and Assistant Head Teachers

PART 11 – Conditions of Employment of Advanced Skills Teachers and Excellent Teachers

PART 12 – Conditions of Employment of Teachers other than Head Teachers

ANNEXES

PART 1 – Commencement and Interpretation

1.1 The provisions of this Document take effect from 1st September 2008.

1.2 In this Document-

"the 2001 Regulations" means the Education (School Teacher Appraisal)(England) Regulations 2001(3) and any reference to "results of the appraisal" within the context of a reference to these Regulations must be construed in accordance with them;

"the 2002 Regulations" means the School Teacher Appraisal (Wales) Regulations 2002(4) and any reference to "appraiser", "appraisal" or "results of the appraisal" within the context of a reference to these Regulations must be construed in accordance with them;

"the 2006 Regulations" means the Education (School Teacher Performance Management) (England) Regulations 2006(5)and any reference to "reviewer", "review", "results of the review" or "planning and review statement" within the context of a reference to these Regulations must be construed in accordance with them;

"the Act" means the Education Act 2002(6);

"advanced skills teacher" means a teacher who holds an advanced skills teacher post;

"advanced skills teacher post" means a post-

(a) in which the post-holder is required–

(i) to be a qualified teacher who, in accordance with an earlier Document, has been certified by an assessor as meeting the standards for advanced skills teachers applicable at the relevant time; or

(ii) to be a qualified teacher who, in accordance with this Document, has satisfied the person to whom the task has been delegated that he meets the core standards, been assessed by an assessor as meeting the post-threshold teacher standards and been certified by that assessor as meeting the excellent teacher standards and the advanced skills teacher standards; or

(3) S.I. 2001/2855.
(4) S.I. 2002/1394.
(5) S.I. 2006/2661.
(6) 2002 c.32.

(iii) to be a post-threshold teacher who, in accordance with this Document, has satisfied the person to whom the task has been delegated that he meets the core standards and the post-threshold teacher standards and been certified by an assessor as meeting the excellent teacher standards and the advanced skills teacher standards; or

(iv) to be an excellent teacher who, in accordance with this Document, has satisfied the person to whom the task has been delegated that he meets the core standards, the post-threshold teacher standards and the excellent teacher standards and been certified by an assessor as meeting the advanced skills teacher standards; and

to undertake one or more of the duties listed in paragraph 68.1 in accordance with paragraph 68.2; and

(b) which has been designated as such either by the relevant body or by the employer in the case of a person employed in the following circumstances-

(i) at an MOD school;

(ii) at an Academy, city technology college or city college for the technology of the arts(7);

(iii) at a non-maintained special school(8);

(iv) by an Education Action Forum(9);

(v) in an establishment maintained by a local authority in the exercise of a social services function; or

(vi) by a person appointed in accordance with a direction made by the Secretary of State under section 497A of the Education Act 1996(10) to perform the functions of an authority and who immediately before such employment was employed by that authority;

(7) Within the meaning of section 482 of the Education Act 1996 (c.56) as originally enacted and as substituted by section 65 of the Act.
(8) Approved in accordance with Regulations (S.I. 1999/2257) made under section 342 of the Education Act 1996.
(9) As established under section 11 of the School Standards and Framework Act 1998 (c.31) as amended by the Act.
(10) Section 497A was inserted in the Education Act 1996 by the School Standards and Framework Act 1998 (c.31) and amended by the Act.

"advanced skills teacher standards" means the professional standards which an advanced skills teacher is required to meet, as set out in Annex 1, where each advanced skills teacher standard is prefixed by the letter 'A';

"assessor" in relation to advanced skills teacher and excellent teacher assessments means an assessor appointed under arrangements made by the Secretary of State under paragraph 31;

"assistant head teacher" means a qualified teacher with leadership responsibilities across the whole school who is appointed to the post of assistant head teacher;

"authority" means a local education authority in England and Wales; and in relation to a school means the authority by which the school is maintained;

"chartered London teacher" means a qualified teacher who has been awarded Chartered London Teacher status in accordance with paragraph 36;

"classroom teacher" means a qualified teacher who is not a member of the leadership group, an excellent teacher or an advanced skills teacher;

"core standards" means the professional standards which all post-threshold teachers, excellent teachers and advanced skills teachers are required to meet, as set out in Annex 1, where each core standard is prefixed by the letter 'C';

"deputy head teacher" means, in relation to England(11), a qualified teacher appointed to the teaching staff of a school as a deputy head teacher in accordance with the School Staffing (England) Regulations 2003(12) and includes a teacher appointed as an acting deputy head teacher but not a teacher who is assigned and carries out the duties of a deputy head teacher without being so appointed;

"earlier Document" means any document referred to in any order made under section 122 of the Act or section 2 of the School Teachers' Pay and Conditions Act 1991(13), other than this Document;

"ERA 1996" means the Employment Rights Act(14);

(11) In relation to Wales, "deputy head teacher" is defined with "head teacher".
(12) S.I. 2003/1963, as amended by S.I. 2003/2725.
(13) 1991 c.49.
(14) 1996 c.18. Part VIII was substituted by Part 1 of Schedule 4 to the Employment Relations Act 1999 (c. 26).

"employment-based teacher training scheme" means in relation to England the scheme established by the Secretary of State under the Education (School Teachers' Qualifications) (England) Regulations 2003([15]), or, in relation to Wales, any scheme established by the National Assembly for Wales under the Education (School Teachers' Qualifications) (Wales) Regulations 2004([16]);

"European Economic Area and Switzerland" means-

(a) the European Community;

(b) subject to the conditions laid down in the EEA Agreement, the area comprising the Republic of Iceland, the Kingdom of Norway and the Principality of Liechtenstein; and

(c) subject to the conditions laid down in the Swiss Agreement, the Swiss Confederation;

"excellent teacher" means a teacher who holds an excellent teacher post;

"excellent teacher post" means a post-

(a) in which the post-holder is required-

  (i) to be a post-threshold teacher who, in accordance with the 2004 Document or any earlier Document, has been assessed as meeting the standards for advanced skills teachers applicable at the relevant time; or

  (ii) to be a post-threshold teacher who has been certified by an assessor as meeting the standards in Annex 2 of the 2005 Document or of the 2006 Document; or

  (iii) to be a post-threshold teacher who in accordance with this Document or the 2007 Document, has satisfied the person to whom the task has been delegated that he meets the core standards and the post-threshold teacher standards and been certified by an assessor as meeting the excellent teacher standards or the advanced skills teacher standards; and

  to undertake the duties listed in paragraph 69; and

(15) S.I. 2003/1662.
(16) S.I. 2004/1729 (W173).

(b) which has been designated as such either by the relevant body or by the employer in the case of a person employed in the following circumstances-

(i) at an MOD school;

(ii) at an Academy, city technology college or city college for the technology of the arts;

(iii) at a non-maintained special school;

(iv) in an establishment maintained by a local authority in the exercise of a social services function; or

(v) by a person appointed in accordance with a direction made by the Secretary of State under section 497A of the Education Act 1996 to perform the functions of an authority and who immediately before such employment was employed by that authority;

"excellent teacher standards" means the professional standards which an excellent teacher is required to meet, as set out in Annex 1, where each excellent teacher standard is prefixed by the letter 'E';

"Fast Track teacher" means a classroom teacher who has been recognised as a Fast Track teacher in accordance with an earlier Document and who has not ceased to be so recognised;

"fifth key stage" means any period of schooling after the completion of the fourth key stage;

"first key stage" means the first key stage as defined in section 82(1)(a) of the Act in relation to England and as defined in section 103(1)(a) of the Act in relation to Wales;

"fourth key stage" means the fourth key stage as defined in section 82(1)(d) of the Act in relation to England and as defined in section 103(1)(d) of the Act in relation to Wales;

"the Fringe Area" means-

(a) in Berkshire- the Districts of Bracknell Forest, Slough and Windsor and Maidenhead;

(b) in Buckinghamshire- the Districts of South Buckinghamshire and Chiltern;

(c) in Essex- the Districts of Basildon, Brentwood, Epping Forest, Harlow and Thurrock;

(d) in Hertfordshire- the Districts of Broxbourne, Dacorum, East Hertfordshire, Hertsmere, St Albans, Three Rivers, Watford and Welwyn Hatfield;

(e) in Kent- the Districts of Dartford and Sevenoaks;

(f) in Surrey- the whole county; and

(g) in West Sussex- the District of Crawley;

"graduate teacher" means in relation to England a teacher who has been granted an authorisation to teach in accordance with paragraphs 5 to 9 of Schedule 2 to the Education (Teachers' Qualifications and Health Standards) (England) Regulations 1999([17]) before 1st September 2002 or in relation to Wales paragraphs 5 to 9 of Schedule 2 to the Education (Teachers' Qualifications and Health Standards) (Wales) Regulations 1999([18]) before 1st September 2004;

"head teacher" means, in relation to England, a person appointed to the teaching staff of a school as head teacher, and includes a person appointed as acting head teacher to carry out the functions of a head teacher pursuant to section 35(3) or 36(3) of the Act but not a teacher who is assigned and carries out duties of a head teacher without being so appointed;

"head teacher" and "deputy head teacher" mean, in relation to Wales, a qualified teacher appointed to the post of head teacher and deputy head teacher respectively in a school, and include a teacher appointed as acting head teacher or deputy head teacher pursuant to section 54 or 55 of, or paragraph 4 of Schedule 16 or paragraph 5 of Schedule 17 to, or regulations made under section 72 of, the School Standards and Framework Act 1998([19]) but not a teacher who is assigned and carries out duties of a head teacher or deputy head teacher without being so appointed;

(17) S.I. 1999/2166, as amended by S.I. 2002/2704, 2001/1391, 2001/2896 and 2001/3737. These Regulations have been revoked by S.I. 2003/1662.
(18) S.I. 1999/2817. Schedule 2 was revoked by S.I. 2004/1744.
(19) 1998 c.31.

"hearing impaired" means deaf or partially hearing;

"individual school range" means the head teacher's pay range determined in accordance with paragraph 12;

"Induction Regulations" means the Education (Induction Arrangements for School Teachers) (England) Regulations 2008([20]) or the Education (Induction Arrangements for School Teachers) (Wales) Regulations 2005([21]);

"Inner London Area" means the area comprising the areas of the London boroughs of Barking and Dagenham, Brent, Camden, City of London, Ealing, Greenwich, Hackney, Hammersmith and Fulham, Haringey, Islington, Kensington and Chelsea, Lambeth, Lewisham, Merton, Newham, Southwark, Tower Hamlets, Wandsworth and Westminster;

"institution of further or higher education" includes an institution providing both further and higher education;

"the London Area" comprises the Inner London Area, the Outer London Area and the Fringe Area;

"member of the leadership group" means a head teacher, a deputy head teacher or an assistant head teacher;

"MOD school" means an educational establishment primarily for children with a parent in the armed forces of the Crown and administered by the Ministry of Defence, other than the educational establishments known as Queen Victoria School, Dunblane and Welbeck College, Loughborough;

"ordinary school" means a school other than a special school;

"the Outer London Area" means Greater London, excluding the Inner London Area;

"post-threshold teacher" means a classroom teacher who-

(a) (i) in accordance with an earlier Document, has been assessed as having met the performance threshold standards throughout the relevant period in accordance with an earlier Document; or

(20) S.I. 2008/657.
(21) S.I. 2005/1813(W.146).

(ii) in accordance with this Document, has satisfied the person to whom the task has been delegated that he meets the core standards and has been assessed by that person as having met the post-threshold teacher standards throughout the relevant period;

(b) at any time prior to his employment as such was employed as a member of the leadership group and in the case of a teacher who was first appointed as such on or after 1st September 2000, occupied such a post or posts for an aggregate period of one year or more;

(c) has held an advanced skills teacher post;

(d) has been certified by an assessor appointed by the Secretary of State as meeting the standards set out in Annex 2 of an earlier Document or the advanced skills teacher standards but who has not been appointed to an advanced skills teacher's post, and would otherwise have been placed on point M6 of the pay scale;

(e) at any time has been employed as a qualified teacher-

(i) in an MOD school;

(ii) by an Education Action Forum;

(iii) at an Academy, city technology college or city college for the technology of the arts;

(iv) at a non-maintained special school;

(v) in an establishment maintained by a local authority in the exercise of a social services function; or

(vi) by a person appointed in accordance with a direction made by the Secretary of State under section 497A of the Education Act 1996 to perform the functions of an authority and who immediately before such employment was employed by that authority;

and whilst employed as such was assessed as meeting all the threshold standards throughout the relevant period provided that, at the date he made his application, he had completed five years of employment (interpreted in accordance with paragraph 1.8) as a qualified teacher;

(f) is appointed as such at a school and has previously been employed for not less than one year by a local education authority as an education adviser or inspector and paid on the Soulbury pay spine;

(g) has been assessed as meeting the sixth form college professional standards;

(h) has been assessed as meeting the Northern Ireland threshold standards; or

(i) has been employed as a qualified teacher otherwise than by a relevant body and during such employment was assessed as meeting all the threshold standards and the assessment was approved by an assessor appointed under arrangements made for that purpose by the Secretary of State;

"post-threshold teacher standards" means the professional standards which a post-threshold teacher is required to meet, as set out in Annex 1, where each post-threshold teacher standard is prefixed by the letter 'P';

"preliminary stage" means any period of schooling prior to the first key stage;

"pupil referral unit" has the meaning given to that expression in section 19(2) of the Education Act 1996([22]);

"qualified teacher" means a person who satisfies requirements specified in regulations under section 132 of the Act([23]);

"registered teacher" means in relation to England a teacher who has been granted an authorisation to teach in accordance with paragraphs 12 to 18 of Schedule 2 to the Education (Teachers' Qualifications and Health Standards) (England) Regulations 1999 before 1st September 2002, or, in relation to Wales, paragraphs 12 to 18 of Schedule 2 to the Education (Teachers' Qualifications and Health Standards)(Wales) Regulations 1999 before 1st September 2004;

"relevant body" means-

(a) in the case of a teacher at a school without a delegated budget, the authority by which that school is maintained,

(22) 1996 c.56.
(23) S.I.2003/1662 (in relation to England) and S.I. 2004/1729 (W173) (in relation to Wales).

(b) in the case of a teacher at a school which has a delegated budget, the governing body of that school, and

(c) in the case of an unattached teacher, the authority by which he is employed;

"relevant period" means the two year period immediately preceding the date of the application for assessment against the post-threshold teacher standards or, where the applicant has not been engaged in the provision of education to children of school age throughout that time, the most recent aggregate period of two years in the five years immediately preceding the date of the application;

"remuneration" means, except where otherwise stated, salary plus any allowances;

"school" means, except where otherwise stated, a school maintained by an authority;

"school causing concern" means a school to which section 15 of the School Standards and Framework Act 1998(24) applies by virtue of subsection (1) (school subject to a formal warning), (4) (school with serious weaknesses) or (6) (school requiring special measures);

"school which has a delegated budget" means a school which has a delegated budget within the meaning of Chapter 1 of Part 3 of the Act, and "school without a delegated budget" must be construed accordingly;

"school year" means a period of 12 months commencing on 1st September unless the school's academic year begins in August in which case it means a period of 12 months commencing on 1st August;

"second key stage" means the second key stage as defined in section 82(1)(b) of the Act in relation to England and as defined in section 103(1)(b) of the Act in relation to Wales;

"SEN allowance" means a special educational needs allowance awarded to a classroom teacher in accordance with paragraph 26;

"Soulbury pay spine" means the pay spine agreed nationally in respect of education advisers and inspectors;

(24) 1998 c.31, as amended by the Learning and Skills Act 2000 (c. 21) and by section 55 of the Act.

"special school" means a special school maintained by an authority;

"Swiss Agreement" means the Agreement, made between the European Community and its Member States of the one part and the Swiss Confederation of the other, on the Free Movement of Persons signed at Luxembourg on 21 June 1999([25]) and which came into force on 1 June 2002;

"teacher" means, except where otherwise stated, a teacher who is a school teacher within the meaning of section 122 of the Act;

"teacher in further or higher education" means a teacher who is-

(a) employed in an institution of further or higher education, or

(b) otherwise employed by a local education authority for the purposes of their functions relating to further and higher education,

other than a teacher seconded to a body which reimburses the employing authority the amount of his salary;

"teacher who has met the Northern Ireland threshold standards" means a teacher who was entitled to be paid on the teachers' upper salary spine as determined by the Department of Education of Northern Ireland under article 69(1) and (6) of the Education and Libraries (Northern Ireland) Order 1986([26]);

"teacher who has met the sixth form college standards" means a teacher who was entitled to the Professional Standards Payment managed by the Sixth Form Colleges' Forum and funded by the Learning and Skills Council;

"the 1988 Document" means the document published by Her Majesty's Stationery Office entitled "School Teachers' Pay and Conditions Document 1988"([27]);

"the 1993 Document" means the document published by Her Majesty's Stationery Office entitled "School Teachers' Pay and Conditions Document 1993"([28]) and includes that document as amended by the Education (School Teachers' Pay and Conditions) Order 1994([29]);

(25) Cmnd. 4904.
(26) S.I.1986/594 (NI3) as amended by S.R. (NI) 1993 No.12.
(27) ISBN 0 11 270654 1.
(28) ISBN 0 11 270843 9.
(29) S.I. 1994/910.

"the 1999 Document" means the document published by Her Majesty's Stationery Office entitled "School Teachers' Pay and Conditions Document 1999"([30]) and includes that document as amended by the Education (School Teachers' Pay and Conditions) Order 2000([31]);

"the 2000 Document" means the document published by Her Majesty's Stationery Office entitled "School Teachers' Pay and Conditions Document 2000"([32]) and includes that document as amended by the Education (School Teachers' Pay and Conditions) (No.3) Order 2000([33]), the Education (School Teachers' Pay and Conditions) (No.4) Order 2000 ([34]), the Education (School Teachers' Pay and Conditions) Order 2001([35]), the Education (School Teachers' Pay and Conditions)(No.2) Order 2001([36]) and the Education (School Teachers' Pay and Conditions)(No.3) Order 2001([37]);

"the 2001 Document" means the document published by Her Majesty's Stationery Office entitled "School Teachers' Pay and Conditions Document 2001"([38]) and includes that document as amended by the Education (School Teachers' Pay and Conditions)(No.6) Order 2001([39]), the Education (School Teachers' Pay and Conditions)(No.7) Order 2001([40]) and the Education (School Teachers' Pay and Conditions) Order 2002([41]);

"the 2004 Document" means the document published by Her Majesty's Stationery Office entitled "School Teachers' Pay and Conditions Document 2004"([42]) and includes that document as amended by the Education (School Teachers' Pay and Conditions) Order 2005([43]) and the Education (School Teachers' Pay and Conditions) (No. 2) Order 2005([44]);

"the 2005 Document" means the document published by Her Majesty's Stationery Office entitled "School Teachers' Pay and Conditions Document 2005"([45]) and includes that document as amended by the Education (School Teachers' Pay and Conditions) (No.4) Order 2005([46]) and the Education (School Teachers' Pay and Conditions) Order 2006([47]);

(30) ISBN 011271069 7.
(31) S.I. 2000/868; revoked by S.I. 2000/2321.
(32) ISBN 011 2710905.
(33) S.I. 2000/2321; revoked by S.I. 2001/2962.
(34) S.I. 2000/3106; revoked by S.I. 2001/2962.
(35) S.I. 2001/720; revoked by S.I. 2001/2962.
(36) S.I. 2001/1254; revoked by S.I. 2001/2962.
(37) S.I. 2001/1284; revoked by S.I. 2001/2962.
(38) ISBN 011 2711073.
(39) S.I. 2001/3243; revoked by S.I. 2002/2223.
(40) S.I. 2001/3435; revoked by S.I. 2002/2223.
(41) S.I. 2002/838; revoked by S.I. 2002/2223.
(42) ISBN 011 2711634.
(43) S.I. 2005/539.
(44) S.I. 2005/1101.
(45) ISBN 011 2711634.
(46) S.I. 2005/3479.
(47) S.I. 2006/1274.

"the 2006 Document" means the document published by Her Majesty's Stationery Office entitled "School Teachers' Pay and Conditions Document 2006"([48]) as amended by the Education (School Teachers' Pay and Conditions) (No. 2) (Amendment) Order 2006([49]) and the Education (School Teachers' Pay and Conditions) (No. 2) (Amendment) Order 2007([50]);

"the 2007 Document" means the document published by Her Majesty's Stationery Office entitled "School Teachers' Pay and Conditions Document 2007"([51]);

"third key stage" means the third key stage as defined in section 82(1)(c) of the Act in relation to England and as defined in section 103(1) (c) of the Act in relation to Wales;

"TLR" means a teaching and learning responsibility payment awarded to a classroom teacher in accordance with paragraph 22;

"unattached teacher" means-

(a) a teacher not attached to a particular school;

(b) a teacher employed otherwise than at a school; or

(c) in Parts 2 to 7, a teacher at a pupil referral unit (including a teacher in charge of a unit);

"unqualified teacher" means a teacher who is not a qualified teacher and who is prescribed by Order under section 122(5) of the Act as a school teacher for the purposes of that section ([52]);

"unlawful discrimination" means, in relation to excellent teacher or advanced skills teacher assessments, any discrimination against a teacher by an assessor, which if the assessor were the relevant body would constitute unlawful discrimination, and "unlawfully discriminate" must be construed accordingly;

"visually impaired" means blind or partially sighted.

1.3 The Interpretation Act 1978([53]) applies to the interpretation of this Document as if it were an Order made under the Act.

(48) ISBN 0-11-271188-X.
(49) S.I. 2006/3171.
(50) S.I. 2007/1688.
(51) ISBN 978-0-11271194-0.
(52) S.I. 2003/1709.
(53) 1978 c.30.

1.4 Where, by or in consequence of a structural or boundary change (or both such changes) as defined in section 14 of the Local Government Act 1992 (54) effected by an order made under section 17 of that Act (as amended), an authority ("the transferor authority") ceases to exercise the functions of an authority in relation to an area and such functions are thereafter exercisable by another authority ("the transferee authority") in relation to that area, the transferor authority and the transferee authority must be regarded, in this Document, as the same authority.

1.5 Where, by virtue of the Local Government (Wales) Act 1994(55), the functions of an abolished authority ("the old authority") under the Education Acts in relation to an area are vested in a new authority in relation to that area ("the new authority"), the old authority and the new authority must be regarded, in this Document, as the same authority.

1.6 Where a table containing a pay scale, pay spine or salary range contains four columns of annual salaries, the column headed "England and Wales (excluding the London Area)" applies to teachers serving in England and Wales except those serving in the London Area, and the column headed "Inner London Area" applies to teachers serving in the Inner London Area, the column headed "Outer London Area" applies to teachers serving in the Outer London Area and the column headed "Fringe Area" applies to teachers serving in the Fringe Area.

1.7 An unqualified teacher who is a head teacher must be treated as a qualified teacher for the purposes of Parts 2 and 3 of this Document.

1.8 For the purposes of Paragraph (e) of the definition of post-threshold teacher and paragraphs 18, 19.3.2(c), 28.2.1(b), 35.1(b), 36.4(a) and 37.7(b)-

(a) a person has completed a "year of employment" if he has completed periods of employment amounting to at least twenty-six weeks in aggregate within the previous school year, in the case of paragraphs 18, 28.2.1(b) and 37.3 or within the previous twelve months in the case of paragraphs 19.3.2(c) and 36.4(a). For these purposes, a period of employment runs from the beginning of the week in which the employment

(54) 1992 c.19.
(55) 1994 c.19.

commences to the end of the week in which the employment is terminated and includes any holiday periods and any periods of absence from work in consequence of sickness or injury, whether the person's service during that period has been full-time or part-time or regular or otherwise;

(b) where a person is absent from work-

(i) in exercise of her right to maternity leave conferred by section 71 or 73 of the ERA 1996([56]) or her contract of employment and has the right to return to work by virtue of those sections or her contract of employment; the right to parental leave conferred by section 76 of the ERA 1996; the right to paternity leave conferred by section 80A, 80AA, 80B or 80BB of the ERA 1996([57]); or the right to adoption leave conferred by section 75A or 75B of the ERA 1996([58]); or

(ii) because of her pregnancy,

the period of absence counts towards the period of service of at least twenty-six weeks referred to in Paragraph (a); and

(c) where a person is absent from work for any reason other than as specified in paragraph 1.8(a) or (b), the relevant body may determine that the period of absence counts as if the person was in employment during it.

1.9 Authorities and governing bodies, in exercising functions and discretions conferred on them by this Document, and persons exercising functions under this Document in accordance with arrangements made by the Secretary of State under paragraph 31 must have regard to any relevant guidance given by the Secretary of State. In applying provisions of this Document authorities and governing bodies must have regard to any guidance about the procedure to be followed given by the Secretary of State.

1.10 Any reference to a numbered sub-paragraph is a reference to the sub-paragraph of that number in the paragraph in which that reference appears, except where otherwise stated.

(56) Sections 71 and 73 were both amended by section 17 of the Employment Act 2002 (c.22) and further amended by paragraphs 31 and 32 of Schedule 1 to the Work and Families Act 2006 (c.18) respectively.

(57) Sections 80A and 80B were inserted by section 1 of 2002 c.22 and sections 80AA and 80BB (which have not, at the time of making these Regulations, been commenced, were inserted by sections 3 and 4 respectively of 2006 c.18.)

(58) Sections 75A and 75B were inserted by section 3 of 2002 c. 22 and amended by paragraphs 33 and 34 of Schedule 1 to 2006 c. 18 respectively.

SECTION 2

PAY
PART 2 – General

Entitlement to salary and allowances

2.1 Subject to paragraphs 43, 44, 46 and 49-

(a) a qualified teacher in full-time service is entitled to remuneration consisting of a salary determined under Part 3 or 4 and any allowances payable to him under Part 4, 6 or 7; and

(b) an unqualified teacher in such service is entitled to remuneration consisting of a salary determined under Part 5 and any allowances payable to him under that Part or Part 6 or 7.

2.2 The relevant body must determine that a graduate teacher, a registered teacher or a teacher on the employment-based teacher training scheme is to-

(a) be paid and be eligible for allowances as a qualified teacher; or

(b) be paid and be eligible for allowances as an unqualified teacher.

2.3 A teacher employed on a part-time basis is entitled to remuneration consisting of a salary and any allowances to which he is entitled calculated in accordance with paragraph 49.

2.4 A teacher employed in a school which has a delegated budget is entitled to be paid by the authority any remuneration to which he is entitled by virtue of the provisions of this Document or any determinations made under it.

Pay policy and grievance procedures

3. The relevant body must-

(a) adopt a policy that sets out the basis on which it determines teachers' pay and the date by which it will determine the teachers' annual pay review; and

(b) in accordance with section 29 of, and Schedule 2 to, the Employment Act 2002([59]), establish procedures for addressing teachers' grievances in relation to their pay.

(59) 2002 c.22.

SECTION 2

Timing of salary determination and notification

4.1 Subject to paragraph 4.3, the determination of the remuneration of a teacher must be made-

(a) annually with effect from 1st September;

(b) whenever a teacher takes up a new post (including taking up a post in the leadership group, as an advanced skills teacher or as an excellent teacher) on a date other than 1st September, with effect from his taking up that post;

(c) where a teacher has been assessed as meeting the post-threshold teacher standards and he is entitled to be paid as a post-threshold teacher pursuant to paragraph 19; or

(d) at any other time when a change falls to be made in a teacher's salary in any circumstances provided for in this Document.

4.2 When determining the remuneration of a teacher, the relevant body must have regard to its pay policy and to the teacher's particular post within its staffing structure.

4.3 Where the relevant body determines to reduce a teacher's remuneration, that determination must take effect no earlier than the date when it was actually made.

4.4 When the relevant body has determined the remuneration of a teacher, it must, at the earliest opportunity and in any event not later than one month after the determination, ensure that the teacher is notified in writing of that determination, of any payments or other financial benefits awarded under paragraph 53, of any safeguarded sums to which he is entitled under paragraphs 21, 25, 27, 35, 38, 40, 46, 47 and 48, where a copy of the school's staffing structure and pay policy may be inspected and-

(a) in the case where the teacher is a member of the leadership group or an advanced skills teacher, of the basis on which his remuneration has been determined and the criteria (including performance objectives where the teacher is not subject to the 2002 Regulations or the 2006 Regulations) on which his salary will be reviewed in the future;

(b) in the case where the teacher was appointed as a member of the leadership group, an advanced skills teacher or an excellent teacher for a fixed period or under a fixed-term contract, of the date or, where appropriate, the circumstance, the occurrence of which will bring the fixed period or fixed-term contract to an end;

(c) in the case where the teacher is a classroom teacher or an unqualified teacher in respect of whom the relevant body has made a determination under paragraph 2.2(a), of-

(i) the number of points awarded under paragraph 17 under each criterion set out in paragraph 18 or, as the case may be, of his position on the pay scale set out in paragraph 19;

(ii) the nature and value of any allowance awarded to him under paragraph 26; and

(iii) in relation to any TLR awarded to him under paragraph 22, its value, the nature of the significant responsibility for which it was awarded and, if the award is made whilst the teacher occupies another post in the temporary absence of the post-holder, the date on which as well as any circumstances in which (if occurring earlier than that date) it will come to an end.

(d) in the case where the teacher is an unqualified teacher to whom paragraph 4.4(c) does not apply, of his position on the unqualified teachers' pay scale determined under paragraph 37, the value of any unqualified teacher's allowance awarded to him under paragraph 38 and the additional responsibility, qualifications or experience in respect of which the allowance was awarded.

4.5 In this paragraph, "remuneration" means salary plus any allowances but does not include any sum paid in respect of the award of Chartered London Teacher status or under paragraphs 51 and 52.

Teachers paid a safeguarded sum

5.1.1 Sub-paragraphs 1.2 and 1.3 apply to a teacher who is paid a safeguarded sum or safeguarded sums under paragraphs 21, 25, 27, 35, 38, 40, 46, 47 and 48.

5.1.2 If the safeguarded sums exceed £500 in total, the relevant body must review the teacher's assigned duties and allocate such additional duties to the teacher as they reasonably consider are appropriate and commensurate with the safeguarded sum, for as long as the teacher continues to be paid the safeguarded sum.

5.1.3 The teacher must not be paid the safeguarded sum if he unreasonably refuses to carry out such additional duties, provided that the teacher is notified of the relevant body's determination to cease paying the safeguarded sum at least one month before it is implemented.

5.2.1 Sub-paragraph 2.2 applies to paragraphs 21, 25, 27, 40, 46 and 47, whenever the relevant body is required to consider whether a point of a higher value ("the new point") or an allowance (including the award of an increase in the value of an allowance made by a decision of the relevant body) ("the new allowance"), or the combined value of a new point and a new allowance, is equal to or exceeds the combined value of a previous pay point and a safeguarded sum.

5.2.2 The relevant body must take into account all the safeguarded sums to which the teacher is entitled and cease paying only the safeguarded sum or combination of safeguarded sums that is equal to or less than the total increase in the teacher's remuneration attributable to the new point or the new allowance.

5.3 For the purposes of paragraphs 25, 35, 38, 47 and 49, the safeguarding period ends on the third anniversary of the relevant date; and in the case of a determination made by the relevant body between –

(a) 1st September and 31st December, the relevant date is 1st January immediately after the end of that period;

(b) 1st January and 31st March, the relevant date is 1st April immediately after the end of that period; and

(c) 1st April and 31st August, the relevant date is 1st September immediately after the end of that period.

PART 3 – Qualified Teachers – Leadership Group Pay

Pay spine for the leadership group

6.1 A head teacher must be paid such salary based upon the leadership group pay spine set out in sub-paragraph 4 as the relevant body determines in accordance with paragraph 7.

6.2 A deputy head teacher must be paid such salary based upon the leadership group pay spine set out in sub-paragraph 4 as the relevant body determines in accordance with paragraph 13.

6.3 An assistant head teacher must be paid such salary based upon the leadership group pay spine set out in sub-paragraph 4 as the relevant body determines in accordance with paragraph 15.

6.4 The pay spine for members of the leadership group is-

Pay Spine for the Leadership Group

Spine point	Annual Salary England and Wales (excluding the London Area)	Annual Salary Inner London Area	Annual Salary Outer London Area	Annual Salary Fringe Area
	£	£	£	£
L1	35,794	42,559	38,634	36,781
L2	36,692	43,460	39,532	37,679
L3	37,608	44,379	40,445	38,594
L4	38,545	45,313	41,388	39,535
L5	39,504	46,278	42,347	40,497
L6	40,494	47,265	43,334	41,484
L7	41,585	48,359	44,428	42,578
L8	42,544	49,315	45,387	43,530
L9	43,607	50,375	46,447	44,597
L10	44,726	51,497	47,569	45,716
L11	45,888	52,653	48,725	46,874
L12	46,945	53,716	49,788	47,938
L13	48,119	54,890	50,962	49,112
L14	49,318	56,089	52,155	50,308
L15	50,547	57,312	53,384	51,531
L16	51,890	58,661	54,730	52,880
L17	53,083	59,854	55,923	54,079
L18	54,417	61,188	57,260	55,406
L19	55,766	62,537	58,609	56,756

Spine point	Annual Salary England and Wales (excluding the London Area)	Annual Salary Inner London Area	Annual Salary Outer London Area	Annual Salary Fringe Area
	£	£	£	£
L20	57,149	63,920	59,992	58,142
L21	58,563	65,334	61,406	59,559
L22	60,017	66,788	62,857	61,009
L23	61,504	68,269	64,344	62,491
L24	63,029	69,800	65,869	64,022
L25	64,596	71,364	67,436	65,583
L26	66,194	72,962	69,034	67,187
L27	67,833	74,600	70,673	68,822
L28	69,517	76,285	72,357	70,504
L29	71,238	78,009	74,078	72,231
L30	73,011	79,782	75,851	73,998
L31	74,816	81,587	77,659	75,808
L32	76,675	83,443	79,515	77,668
L33	78,581	85,349	81,424	79,573
L34	80,523	87,294	83,366	81,516
L35	82,524	89,295	85,364	83,517
L36	84,568	91,336	87,405	85,558
L37	86,670	93,444	89,513	87,660
L38	88,815	95,583	91,655	89,805
L39	90,979	97,747	93,819	91,966
L40	93,250	100,024	96,093	94,243
L41	95,580	102,354	98,423	96,570
L42	97,974	104,742	100,811	98,967
L43	100,424	107,192	103,264	101,417

Pay Spine for the Leadership Group

Annual determination of a head teacher's salary

7.1 This paragraph applies for the purpose of the determination of a head teacher's salary.

7.2 For the purpose of determining the salary of a head teacher who is not subject to the 2002 Regulations or the 2006 Regulations -

(a) the relevant body and the head teacher must seek to agree performance objectives relating to school leadership and management and pupil progress, and in default of agreement the relevant body must set such performance objectives; and

(b) the relevant body must review the performance of the head teacher taking account of the performance objectives agreed or set under sub-paragraph 2(a).

7.3 The relevant body must determine the salary of a head teacher in accordance with the following-

(a) subject to paragraphs 47 and 48, a head teacher's salary must not be less than the minimum of the individual school range and must not exceed the maximum of the individual school range;

(b) save to the extent that movement up the pay spine is necessary to ensure that the salary of the head teacher equals the minimum of the individual school range, there must not be any movement up the pay spine unless-

(i) in the case where the head teacher is not subject to the 2002 Regulations or the 2006 Regulations, a review of his performance has been carried out under sub-paragraph 2(b)and there has been a sustained high quality of performance by him, having regard to the performance objectives agreed or set under sub-paragraph 2(a); or

(ii) where the head teacher is subject to the 2002 Regulations or the 2006 Regulations, there has been a sustained high quality of performance by him, having regard to the results of the most recent appraisal carried out in accordance with the 2002 Regulations or the results of the most recent review carried out in accordance with the 2006 Regulations, as the case may be;

(c) when making any determination under Paragraph (b) in the case of a head teacher who is subject to the 2006 Regulations, the relevant body must have regard to any recommendation on pay progression recorded in the head teacher's most recent planning and review statement;

(d) save to the extent that a movement up the pay spine is necessary to ensure that the salary of the head teacher equals the minimum of the individual school range, a head teacher's salary must not be increased by more than two points in the course of one school year;

(e) a newly appointed head teacher must not on his appointment be paid at a point exceeding the third point above the minimum of the individual school range;

(f) where the relevant body raises the individual school range, any performance points awarded by the relevant body for the previous year must be calculated on the basis of the lower individual school range before the head teacher's pay is assimilated onto the higher range; and

(g) where in accordance with paragraph 12.2.6 the relevant body determines an individual school range the maximum of which exceeds the highest point on the leadership group pay spine, it must determine the value of each point above the highest point.

Determination of the school's head teacher group

8.1 The relevant body must assign its school to a head teacher group for the purposes of paragraph 12 in accordance with this paragraph and paragraphs 9, 10 and 11.

8.2 A school must be assigned to a head teacher group whenever the relevant body sees fit.

8.3 The head teacher groups, and pay ranges in relation thereto, are as follows-

Head Teacher Groups and Pay Ranges

Group	Range of spine points	Annual Salary Range England and Wales (excluding the London Area)	Annual Salary Range Inner London Area	Annual Salary Range Outer London Area	Annual Salary Range Fringe Area
		£	£	£	£
1	L6-L18	40,494 – 54,417	47,265 – 61,188	43,334 – 57,260	41,484 – 55,406
2	L8-L21	42,544 – 58,563	49,315 – 65,334	45,387 – 61,406	43,530 – 59,559

Head Teacher Groups and Pay Ranges

Group	Range of spine points	Annual Salary Range England and Wales (excluding the London Area)	Annual Salary Range Inner London Area	Annual Salary Range Outer London Area	Annual Salary Range Fringe Area
		£	£	£	£
3	L11-L24	45,888 – 63,029	52,653 – 69,800	48,725 – 65,869	46,874 – 64,022
4	L14-L27	49,318 – 67,833	56,089 – 74,600	52,155 – 70,673	50,308 – 68,822
5	L18-L31	54,417 – 74,816	61,188 – 81,587	57,260 – 77,659	55,406 – 75,808
6	L21-L35	58,563 – 82,524	65,334 – 89,295	61,406 – 85,364	59,559 – 83,517
7	L24-L39	63,029 – 90,979	69,800 – 97,747	65,869 – 93,819	64,022 – 91,966
8	L28-L43	69,517 – 100,424	76,285 – 107,192	72,357 – 103,264	70,504 – 101,417

Unit totals and head teacher groups – ordinary schools

9.1 Subject to paragraph 11, an ordinary school must be assigned to a head teacher group in accordance with the following table by reference to its total unit score calculated in accordance with sub-paragraph 2-

Total unit score	*School group*
Up to 1,000	1
1,001 to 2,200	2
2,201 to 3,500	3
3,501 to 5,000	4
5,001 to 7,500	5
7,501 to 11,000	6
11,001 to 17,000	7
17,001 and over	8

SECTION 2

9.2 Subject to sub-paragraph 3, the total unit score must be determined in accordance with the number of pupils on the school register, calculated as follows-

Key Stage	*Units per pupil*
For each pupil in the preliminary stage and each pupil in the first or second key stage	7
For each pupil in the third key stage	9
For each pupil in the fourth key stage	11
For each pupil in the fifth key stage	13

9.3.1 The number of pupils on the school register, and the number of pupils at each key stage, must be determined by the numbers as shown on the most recent return of the Department for Children, Schools and Families Annual School Census, or the most recently available Welsh Assembly Government Annual School Census[60], submitted to the Department for Children, Schools and Families or Welsh Assembly Government respectively on behalf of the school;

9.3.2 Each pupil with a statement of special educational needs must, if he is in a special class consisting wholly or mainly of such pupils, be counted as three units more than he would otherwise be counted as by virtue of sub-paragraph 2, and if he is not in such a special class be counted as three such units only where the relevant body so determines;

9.3.3 Each pupil who attends for no more than half a day on each day for which he attends the school must be counted as half as many units as he would otherwise be counted as under sub-paragraphs 2 or 3.2.

Unit totals and head teacher groups – special schools

10.1 Subject to paragraph 11, a special school must be assigned to a head teacher group in accordance with the following table by reference to its modified total unit score calculated in accordance with sub-paragraphs 2 to 5-

(60) This form relates to schools in Wales.

Modified total unit score	*School group*
Up to 2,200	2
2,201 to 3,500	3
3,501 to 5,000	4
5,001 to 7,500	5
7,501 to 11,000	6
11,001 to 17,000	7
17,001 and over	8

10.2 The relevant body must calculate the proportion of staff to pupils at the school expressed as a percentage ("the staff-pupil ratio") in accordance with the following formula-

$$\frac{A}{B} \times 100$$

where A is the number of teachers and support staff weighted as provided in sub-paragraph 2.1, and B is the number of pupils at the school weighted as provided in sub-paragraph 2.2.

10.2.1 The weighting for a teacher is two units for each full-time equivalent teacher, and the weighting for each support staff member is one unit for each full-time equivalent individual.

10.2.2 The weighting for a full-time pupil is one unit and the weighting for a part-time pupil is half a unit.

10.3 The relevant body must calculate the staff- pupil ratio modifier in accordance with the following table by reference to the staff-pupil ratio determined in accordance with sub-paragraph 2-

Staff-pupil ratio	*Staff-pupil ratio modifier*
1 – 20%	1
21 – 35%	2
36 – 50%	3
51 – 65%	4
66 – 80%	5
81% or more	6

10.4 The relevant body must determine the school's total unit score in accordance with the number of pupils on the school register calculated as follows-

Key Stage	*Units per pupil*
For each pupil in the preliminary stage and each pupil in the first or second key stage	10
For each pupil in the third key stage	12
For each pupil in the fourth key stage	14
For each pupil in the fifth key stage	16

10.5 The relevant body must determine the school's modified total unit score by multiplying the school's total unit score determined under sub-paragraph 4 by the staff-pupil ratio modifier calculated under sub-paragraph 3.

10.6 In this paragraph-

(a) the number of pupils on the school register must be determined by the numbers as shown on the most recent return of the Department for Children, Schools and Families Annual School Census, or the most recently available National Assembly for Wales Form STATS 2([61]), submitted to the Department for Children, Schools and Families or National Assembly for Wales respectively on behalf of the school; and

(b) "support staff member" means a member of the school staff who is not-

(i) a teacher;

(ii) a person employed in connection with the provision of meals;

(iii) a person employed in connection with the security or maintenance of the school premises; or

(iv) a person employed in a residential school to supervise and care for pupils out of school hours.

(61) This form relates to schools in Wales.

Unit totals and head teacher groups – particular cases

Expected changes in number of registered pupils and teaching establishments

11.1.1 Subject to sub-paragraph 1.2, where in the case of an ordinary school the total unit score and in the case of a special school the modified total unit score is expected by the relevant body to rise or fall after the date to which the assignment refers, the relevant body may instead assign the school to the appropriate group which would result after the expected change in numbers has taken place.

11.1.2 Where the relevant body is the governing body of a school which has a delegated budget, no assignment must be made until the authority has been consulted.

New schools

11.2.1 Subject to sub-paragraphs 2.2 and 2.3, in the case of a school which is newly opened or not yet open, the relevant body must assign the school to the group appropriate in the case of an ordinary school to the total unit score and in the case of a special school to the modified total unit score expected by the authority or, in the case of a school with a delegated budget, by the governing body after consulting the authority to be relevant not less than four years from the date of opening.

11.2.2 The relevant body must, as necessary, revise its assignment as the expectations on which its calculation was based change.

11.2.3 Where the relevant body is the governing body of a school which has a delegated budget, no assignment must be made until the authority has been consulted.

Determination of a school's individual school range

12.1.1 The relevant body must determine a school's individual school range in accordance with sub-paragraph 2.

12.1.2 The individual school range must consist of seven consecutive spine points, and where the maximum of the individual school range exceeds the maximum of the leadership group pay spine, the relevant body must determine the level of any pay points above the spine maximum.

12.2.1 The minimum of the individual school range must not be less than the minimum of the range specified in paragraph 8.3 in relation to the school's head teacher group ("the head teacher group range").

12.2.2 Subject to sub-paragraphs 2.3 to 2.6, the maximum of the individual school range must not exceed the maximum of the head teacher group range.

12.2.3 The relevant body must ensure that the minimum of the individual school range-

(a) is at least the next point higher on the leadership group scale than the maximum of the pay range of any deputy or assistant head teacher at the school; and

(b) is not less than the next leadership group pay spine point above the salary of the highest paid classroom teacher (calculated in accordance with sub-paragraph 3).

12.2.4 Where the relevant body is required to raise an individual school range by virtue of sub-paragraph 2.3, it must raise it by no more than is necessary to secure that the minimum of the individual school range exceeds by one point the maximum of the deputy or assistant head teacher range or the salary of the highest paid classroom teacher (as the case may be).

12.2.5 The relevant body may determine the individual school range in accordance with sub-paragraph 2.6 where-

(a) the school is a school causing concern;

(b) if the maximum of the individual school range did not exceed the maximum of the head teacher group range, the relevant body consider the school would have substantial difficulty filling the vacant head teacher post; or

(c) if the maximum of the individual school range did not exceed the maximum of the head teacher group range, the relevant body consider the school would have substantial difficulty retaining the existing head teacher.

12.2.6 In the circumstances described in sub-paragraph 2.5 the relevant body may determine an individual school range which exceeds the head teacher group range, but the maximum of the individual school range so determined must not exceed the maximum of the second head teacher group range above the appropriate head teacher group range. If the appropriate head teacher group is group 7 or 8, the individual school range must be such as the relevant body determines, and its maximum may exceed the highest point on the leadership group pay spine.

12.3.1 For the purpose of determining the individual school range, a deputy head teacher's pay range or an assistant head teacher's pay range, the relevant body must calculate the salary of the highest paid classroom teacher in accordance with sub-paragraph 3.2.

12.3.2 The salary of the highest paid classroom teacher is the sum of-

(a) the value of point 1 on the upper pay scale;

(b) the value of any TLR awarded to the highest paid classroom teacher at the school under paragraph 22; and

(c) the value of any SEN allowance awarded to the highest paid classroom teacher at the school under paragraph 26.

12.3.3 In sub-paragraph 3.2, the highest paid classroom teacher at the school is the classroom teacher with the highest allowance total, being the total value of any TLR or SEN allowance awarded to him.

12.3.4 The calculation of the salary of the highest paid classroom teacher for the purpose of Part 3 is a notional calculation and must not affect the salary entitlement of such a teacher.

Annual determination of a deputy head teacher's salary

13.1 This paragraph applies for the purpose of determining a deputy head teacher's salary.

13.2 For the purpose of determining the salary of a deputy head teacher who is not subject to the 2002 Regulations or the 2006 Regulations-

13.2.1 the relevant body and the deputy head teacher must seek to agree performance objectives relating to school leadership and management and pupil progress, and in default of agreement the relevant body must set such performance objectives; and

13.2.2 the relevant body must review the performance of the deputy head teacher having regard to the performance objectives agreed or set under sub-paragraph 2.1.

13.3 The relevant body must determine the salary of a deputy head teacher in accordance with the following-

(a) save to the extent that a movement up the pay spine is necessary to ensure that the salary of the deputy head teacher equals the minimum of his deputy head teacher pay range, there must not be any movement up the pay spine unless-

(i) in the case where the deputy head teacher is not subject to the 2002 Regulations or the 2006 Regulations, a review of his performance has been carried out under sub-paragraph 2.2 and there has been a sustained high quality of performance by him, having regard to the performance objectives agreed or set under sub-paragraph 2.1; or

(ii) where the deputy head teacher is subject to the 2002 Regulations or the 2006 Regulations, there has been a sustained high quality of performance by him, having regard to the results of the most recent appraisal carried out in accordance with the 2002 Regulations or the results of the most recent review carried out in accordance with the 2006 Regulations, as the case may be;

(b) when making any determination under Paragraph (a) in the case of a deputy head teacher who is subject to the 2006 Regulations, the relevant body must have regard to any recommendation on pay progression recorded in the teacher's most recent planning and review statement.

(c) a deputy head teacher's salary must not be less than the minimum of his deputy head teacher pay range and must not exceed the maximum of that range;

(d) save to the extent that a movement up the pay spine is necessary to ensure that the salary of the deputy head teacher equals the minimum of his deputy head teacher pay range, his salary must not be increased by more than two points in the course of one school year;

(e) where the relevant body raises a deputy head teacher's pay range, any performance points awarded by the relevant body for the previous year must be calculated on the basis of the lower pay range before the deputy head teacher's pay is assimilated onto the higher pay range.

13.4 A newly appointed deputy head teacher must not on his appointment be paid at a point exceeding the second point above the minimum of his deputy head teacher pay range.

Determination of a deputy head teacher's pay range

14.1.1 The relevant body must determine a deputy head teacher pay range for each deputy head teacher in accordance with sub-paragraph 2.

14.1.2 A deputy head teacher's pay range must consist of five consecutive spine points on the leadership group pay spine.

14.2.1 When a deputy head teacher's pay range is determined pursuant to sub-paragraph 1.1, the relevant body must ensure that the minimum of the deputy head teacher's pay range is not less than the next leadership group pay spine point above-

(a) the salary of the highest paid classroom teacher (calculated in accordance with paragraph 12.3); and

(b) the minimum of the assistant head teacher's pay range of the highest paid assistant head teacher at the school.

14.2.2 When a deputy head teacher's pay range is determined pursuant to sub-paragraph 1.1, the relevant body must ensure that the maximum of the deputy head teacher's pay range does not equal or exceed the minimum of the individual school range.

14.2.3 Where there is insufficient space on the leadership group pay spine to accommodate a deputy head teacher's pay range of five points between the salary of the highest paid classroom teacher or the minimum of an assistant head teacher pay range and the minimum of the individual school range, the individual school range must be raised to the extent necessary to accommodate the deputy head teacher's pay range.

14.2.4 Subject to sub-paragraphs 2.1 and 2.3, the relevant body must not determine a deputy head teacher's pay range at so high a level that they are required by virtue of any other provision of this Document to raise the individual school range beyond the maximum of the head teacher group range.

Annual determination of an assistant head teacher's salary

15.1 This paragraph applies for the purpose of determining an assistant head teacher's salary.

15.2 For the purpose of determining the salary of an assistant head teacher who is not subject to the 2002 Regulations or the 2006 Regulations-

(a) the relevant body and the assistant head teacher must seek to agree performance objectives relating to school leadership and management and pupil progress, and in default of agreement the relevant body must set such performance objectives; and

(b) the relevant body must review the performance of the assistant head teacher taking account of the performance objectives agreed or set under sub-paragraph 2(a).

15.3 The relevant body must determine the salary of an assistant head teacher in accordance with the following-

(a) save to the extent that a movement up the pay spine is necessary to ensure that the salary of the assistant head teacher equals the minimum of his assistant head teacher pay range, there must not be any movement up the pay spine unless-

(i) in the case where the assistant head teacher is not subject to the 2002 Regulations or the 2006 Regulations, a review of his performance has been carried out under sub-paragraph 2(b) and there has been a sustained high quality of performance by him, having regard to the performance objectives agreed or set under sub-paragraph 2(a); or

(ii) where the assistant head teacher is subject to the 2002 Regulations or the 2006 Regulations, there has been a sustained high quality of performance by him, having regard to the results of the most recent appraisal carried out in accordance with the 2002 Regulations or the results of the most recent review carried out in accordance with the 2006 Regulations, as the case may be;

(b) when making any determination under Paragraph (a) in the case of an assistant head teacher who is subject to the 2006 Regulations, the relevant body must have regard to any recommendation on pay progression recorded in the teacher's most recent planning and review statement.

(c) an assistant head teacher's salary must not be less than the minimum of his assistant head teacher's pay range and must not exceed the maximum of that range;

(d) save to the extent that a movement up the pay spine is necessary to ensure that the salary of the assistant head teacher equals the minimum of his assistant head teacher pay range, his salary must not be increased by more than two points in the course of one school year;

(e) where the relevant body raises an assistant head teacher's pay range, any performance points awarded by the relevant body for the previous year must be calculated on the basis of the lower pay range before the assistant head teacher's pay is assimilated onto the higher pay range.

15.4 A newly appointed assistant head teacher must not on his appointment be paid at a point exceeding the second point above the minimum of his assistant head teacher pay range.

Determination of an assistant head teacher's pay range

16.1.1 The relevant body must determine an assistant head teacher pay range for each assistant head teacher in accordance with sub-paragraph 2.

16.1.2 An assistant head teacher's pay range must consist of five consecutive spine points on the leadership group pay spine.

16.2.1 When an assistant head teacher's pay range is determined pursuant to sub-paragraph 1.1, the relevant body must ensure that the minimum of the assistant head teacher's pay range is not less than the next leadership group pay spine point above the salary of the highest paid classroom teacher (calculated in accordance with paragraph 12.3).

16.2.2 When an assistant head teacher's pay range is determined pursuant to sub-paragraph 1.1, the relevant body must ensure that the maximum of the assistant head teacher's pay range does not equal or exceed-

(a) the minimum of the individual school range; or

(b) where the school has one or more deputy head teachers, the maximum of the deputy head teacher pay range of the lowest paid deputy head teacher.

16.2.3 Where there is insufficient space on the leadership group pay spine to accommodate an assistant head teacher's pay range of five points between the salary of the highest paid classroom teacher and the minimum of the individual school range (and where applicable, in addition to accommodate a deputy head teacher pay range of any deputy head teacher at the school in accordance with paragraphs 14.2.1 and sub-paragraph 2.2(b)the individual school range must be raised to the extent necessary to accommodate the assistant head teacher's pay range.

16.2.4 Subject to sub-paragraphs 2.1 and 2.3, the relevant body must not determine an assistant head teacher's pay range at so high a level that it is required by virtue of any other provision of this Document to raise the individual school range beyond the maximum of the head teacher group range.

PART 4 – Other Qualified Teachers

Pay scale for classroom teachers

17.1 This paragraph and paragraph 18 apply to a classroom teacher who is not a post-threshold teacher, and references to "classroom teacher" in this paragraph and paragraph 18 must be construed accordingly.

17.2 A classroom teacher must be paid such salary based on the pay scale set out in sub-paragraph 3 as the relevant body determines in accordance with sub-paragraph 4 and paragraph 39.

17.3 The pay scale for classroom teachers is-

Pay Scale for Classroom Teachers

Scale point	Annual Salary England and Wales (excluding the London Area)	Annual Salary Inner London Area	Annual Salary Outer London Area	Annual Salary Fringe Area
	£	£	£	£
M1	20,627	25,000	24,000	21,619
M2	22,259	26,581	25,487	23,248
M3	24,048	28,261	27,065	25,037
M4	25,898	30,047	28,741	26,894
M5	27,939	32,358	31,178	28,931
M6	30,148	34,768	33,554	31,138

17.4 Subject to paragraphs 28 and 39, the relevant body must determine the point above the minimum point on the pay scale in sub-paragraph 3 on which each individual classroom teacher is to be placed in accordance with paragraph 18 only. If a classroom teacher is not entitled to any points in accordance with paragraph 18, he must be placed at the minimum point on the pay scale.

Mandatory Points

18.1.1 The relevant body must award-

(a) the number of points awarded when the classroom teacher was first placed on the pay scale for classroom teachers in accordance with any of the Documents published between 2002 and 2007 or paragraph 28 of this Document;

SECTION 2

(b) a point for each year of employment (interpreted in accordance with paragraph 1.8) as a classroom teacher completed since he was first so placed unless the teacher has been notified in writing in accordance with sub-paragraph 1.6 that his service has not been satisfactory in respect of any such year.

18.1.2 Subject to sub-paragraph 3.2, the relevant body must award a point for each year of employment as a qualified teacher-

(a) at an MOD school; or

(b) by an Education Action Forum.

18.1.3 Subject to sub-paragraph 3.2, in the case of a classroom teacher who is a qualified teacher by virtue of regulation 5(b) of, and paragraph 8 of Schedule 2 to, the Education (School Teachers' Qualifications) (England) Regulations 2003(62), or by virtue of regulation 5(a) of and paragraph 4 of Schedule 2 to, the Education (School Teachers' Qualifications) (Wales) Regulations 2004(63), the relevant body must award a point for each year of employment as a person qualified to teach school age children within state sector schools in the European Economic Area and Switzerland (other than in England and Wales).

18.1.4 Subject to sub-paragraph 3.2, in the case of a classroom teacher other than one to whom sub-paragraph 1.3 applies, the relevant body must award a point for each year of employment as a person qualified to teach school age children within state sector schools in the European Economic Area and Switzerland (other than in England and Wales).

18.1.5 The relevant body must award a point to a person appointed as a Fast Track teacher who was assessed as meeting the standards for Fast Track teachers under an earlier Document and who is first placed on the pay scale for classroom teachers under this Document.

18.1.6 Where a classroom teacher remains in service on 1st September in the school in which he was employed during the previous school year, the relevant body, when considering whether or not his service has been satisfactory for the purposes of sub-paragraph 1.1(b), must seek and take into account advice from the head teacher and where the relevant body considers that the classroom teacher's service has been unsatisfactory it must notify the teacher in writing before the

(62) S.I. 2003/1662
(63) S.I. 2004/1729 (W.173).

end of the current school year and before the relevant body makes a determination for the purpose of sub-paragraph 1.1.

Discretionary Points

18.2.1 Subject to sub-paragraph 3.2, the relevant body may award-

(a) 1 point to a classroom teacher who has been notified that a year of employment has not been satisfactory, in respect of that year;

(b) 1 or more points for years of experience other than employment as a classroom teacher which the relevant body considers to be of value to the performance of the classroom teacher's duties;

(c) in a case to which paragraph 4.1(a) applies, 1 point-

(i) where the teacher is not subject to the 2002 Regulations or the 2006 Regulations, his performance in the previous school year was excellent, having regard to all aspects of his professional duties, in particular, classroom teaching; or

(ii) where the teacher is subject to the 2002 Regulations or the 2006 Regulations, his performance in the previous school year was excellent, having regard to the results of the most recent appraisal carried out in accordance with the 2002 Regulations or the most recent review carried out in accordance with the 2006 Regulations, as the case may be.

18.2.2 When making any determination in accordance with sub-paragraph 2.1(c)(ii) in the case of a classroom teacher who is subject to the 2006 Regulations, the relevant body must have regard to any recommendation on pay progression recorded in the teacher's most recent planning and review statement.

18.3.1 Points awarded under sub-paragraphs 1 or 2 must be permanent, whether the classroom teacher remains in the same post, or takes up a new one.

18.3.2 In making an award under sub-paragraph 1.2, 1.3, 1.4 or 2, the relevant body must not take into account years of employment for which the classroom teacher has previously been awarded points under sub-paragraph 1.1(a).

SECTION 2

Post-threshold teachers

Pay scale for post-threshold teachers

19.1 A post-threshold teacher must be paid such salary based on the pay scale set out in sub-paragraph 2 as the relevant body determines, subject to sub-paragraphs 3 to 5.

19.2 The pay scale for post-threshold teachers is-

Pay Scale for Post-Threshold Teachers

Scale point	**Annual Salary England and Wales (excluding the London Area)**	**Annual Salary Inner London Area**	**Annual Salary Outer London Area**	**Annual Salary Fringe Area**
	£	£	£	£
U1	32,660	39,114	35,926	33,652
U2	33,870	41,035	37,257	34,860
U3	35,121	42,419	38,634	36,114

19.3.1 Subject to sub-paragraphs 3.2 to 3.5, when a teacher first becomes entitled to be paid as a post-threshold teacher, the relevant body must determine that he is to be paid on scale point U1 on the pay scale set out in sub-paragraph 2 with effect from 1st September in the following school year.

19.3.2 The determination must have effect from 1st September in the school year in which the teacher made his application for assessment against the threshold standards if either-

(a) the application is his first application for assessment against the threshold standards and he was placed either at point M6 of the main pay scale or on the leadership pay spine in any previous school year;

(b) the application is not his first application and he was placed at point M6 of the main pay scale before 1st September 2007; or

(c) the teacher was employed as a qualified teacher otherwise than by a relevant body in the school year preceding the year in which he made his application and he had completed at least six years of employment (interpreted in accordance with paragraph 1.8) as a qualified teacher at the date he made his application.

19.3.3 Where a teacher who becomes a post-threshold teacher via any of the routes referred to in Paragraph (b), (c), (e), (f), (g), (h) or (i) of the definition of post-threshold teacher in paragraph 1.2 becomes entitled to be paid as a post-threshold teacher (whether for the first time or a subsequent time), the relevant body must determine the point on the pay scale set out in sub-paragraph 2 on which he is to be paid.

19.4.1 Save in exceptional circumstances, there must be no movement up the pay scale set out in sub-paragraph 2 prior to the second annual determination after the date on which the post-threshold teacher was first placed on that scale or the date on which the teacher was last awarded an additional point on that scale unless-

(a) in the case where the post-threshold teacher is not subject to the 2002 Regulations or the 2006 Regulations, there has first been a review of his performance and the relevant body is satisfied that the teacher's achievements and contribution to the school, or to the school or schools in which he previously worked, have been substantial and sustained; or

(b) in the case where the post-threshold teacher is subject to the 2002 Regulations or the 2006 Regulations, the relevant body is satisfied that the teacher's achievements and contribution to the school, or to the school or schools in which he previously worked have been substantial and sustained, having regard to the results of the two most recent appraisals or reviews carried out in accordance with the 2001 Regulations, the 2002 Regulations or the 2006 Regulations, as the case may be.

19.4.2 When making any determination under sub-paragraph 4.1 in the case of a post-threshold teacher who is subject to the 2006 Regulations, the relevant body must have regard to any recommendatlon on pay progression recorded in the teacher's most recent planning and review statement.

19.5 A post-threshold teacher's salary must not be increased by more than one scale point in the course of a single annual salary determination and any such points must be permanent whether the teacher remains in the same post or takes up a new one.

Assessment against post-threshold teacher standards

20.1 A qualified teacher ("the applicant") may apply once in any school year to the relevant body for assessment against the post-threshold teacher standards when, or at any time after, he has been placed on point M6 of the pay scale set out in paragraph 17.3.

20.2 Where an applicant is employed to teach at more than one school he may not apply to the relevant body of more than one such school.

20.3.1 Except where the applicant is an unattached teacher, the relevant body must delegate the receipt and assessment of the application to the head teacher.

20.3.2 Where the applicant is an unattached teacher, the relevant body must delegate the receipt and assessment of the application to a person with management responsibility for the applicant.

20.4 The application must contain a summary of the evidence the teacher wishes to rely on in order to demonstrate that he has met the post-threshold teacher standards throughout the relevant period.

20.5 Prior to carrying out the assessment against the post-threshold teacher standards, the person to whom the task of assessing the application has been delegated must be satisfied that the applicant meets the core standards, and, in the case where the teacher is subject to the 2002 Regulations or the 2006 Regulations, the person to whom the task has been delegated must have regard to the results of the most recent appraisal carried out in accordance with the 2002 Regulations or the most recent review carried out in accordance with the 2006 Regulations, as the case may be.

20.6 Where the person to whom the task of assessing the application has been delegated is not satisfied that the applicant meets the core standards, he must reject the application and inform the applicant, giving reasons.

20.7 Where the person to whom the task of assessing the application has been delegated is satisfied that the applicant meets the core standards, he must go on to carry out the assessment against the post-threshold teacher standards.

20.8 When carrying out the assessment against the post-threshold teacher standards the person to whom the task has been delegated must have regard to the evidence mentioned in the application and, in the case where the teacher is subject to the 2002 Regulations or the 2006 Regulations, the results of the most recent appraisal carried out in accordance with the 2002 Regulations or the results of the most recent review carried out in accordance with the 2006 Regulations, as the case may be.

20.9 Having carried out the assessment under sub-paragraph 8, the person to whom the task of assessing the application has been delegated must determine whether the applicant has met the post-threshold teacher standards throughout the relevant period and inform the applicant of his decision, giving reasons in the case where he determines that the applicant has not met the standards.

Allowances for classroom teachers

Safeguarding management allowances

21.1 Except in relation to a teacher who is paid a management allowance as part of a safeguarded salary under paragraph 45, this paragraph applies to a teacher who was awarded a management allowance under an earlier Document.

21.2 Subject to paragraphs 5.1, 5.2 and sub-paragraphs 3 and 4, the teacher must be paid the safeguarded sum from 1st January 2006 until–

(a) 31st December 2008;

(b) if the safeguarded sum is paid in respect of a management allowance that was awarded for a fixed period, that period expires;

(c) the teacher ceases to be a classroom teacher;

(d) the teacher is placed on a higher point on either the pay scale set out in paragraph 17.3 or in paragraph 19.2, or he first becomes entitled to be paid on the pay scale set out in paragraph 19.2 as a result of a pay determination that has effect after 1st September 2008; and the combined value of that point and any TLR awarded to him equals or exceeds the combined value of his original salary and the safeguarded sum; or

(e) the teacher's employment at the school ends other than in circumstances to which paragraph 45 or 46 applies, whichever is the first to occur.

21.3 The safeguarded sum must be reduced by the value of any TLR awarded to the teacher by the relevant body from time to time and, in the case where the TLR is awarded to a teacher whilst he occupies another post in the temporary absence of the post-holder, restored upon the expiry of the period of that award, unless, in the meantime, any of the events specified in sub-paragraph 2 occurs.

21.4 Payment of the safeguarded sum must be discontinued whilst the teacher occupies a post as a member of the leadership group, as an advanced skills teacher or as an excellent teacher in the temporary absence of the post-holder but reinstated thereafter, unless, in the meantime, any of the events specified in sub-paragraph 2 occurs.

21.5 In this paragraph-

(a) "original salary" means the value at 31st December 2005 of the point at which the teacher was placed on the pay scale set out in paragraph 17.3 or in paragraph 19.2 of the 2005 Document, taking into account the annual determination required by paragraph 4.1 of that Document;

(b) "safeguarded sum" means the value at 31st December 2005 of the management allowance.

Teaching and learning responsibility payments

22.1. The relevant body may award a TLR to a classroom teacher for undertaking a sustained additional responsibility in the context of their staffing structure for the purpose of ensuring the continued delivery of high-quality teaching and learning and for which he is made accountable. The award may be while a teacher remains in the same post or occupies another post in the temporary absence of the post-holder, in accordance with and subject to paragraph 3 and sub-paragraphs 2 to 4.

22.2 Having decided to award a TLR, the relevant body must determine whether to award a first TLR ("TLR1") or a second TLR ("TLR2") and its value, in accordance with their pay policy, provided that–

(a) the annual value of a TLR1 must be no less than £6,997 and no greater than £11,841;

(b) the annual value of a TLR2 must be no less than £2,422 and no greater than £5,920; and

(c) if the relevant body awards TLRs of different annual values to two or more teachers, the minimum difference in the annual value between each award of a TLR1 is £1,500 and between each award of a TLR2 is £1,500.

22.3 Before awarding a TLR the relevant body must be satisfied that the teacher's duties include a significant responsibility that is not required of all classroom teachers and that–

(a) is focused on teaching and learning;

(b) requires the exercise of a teacher's professional skills and judgement;

(c) requires the teacher to lead, manage and develop a subject or curriculum area; or to lead and manage pupil development across the curriculum;

(d) has an impact on the educational progress of pupils other than the teacher's assigned classes or groups of pupils; and

(e) involves leading, developing and enhancing the teaching practice of other staff.

22.4 In addition, before awarding a TLR1, the relevant body must be satisfied that the significant responsibility referred to in sub-paragraph 3 includes line management responsibility for a significant number of people.

Increase of teaching and learning responsibility payments in payment

23.1 This paragraph applies to a TLR awarded to a classroom teacher prior to 1st September 2008 to which he remains entitled on that date.

23.2 Subject to paragraph 22.2, the amount of the TLR must be increased by the relevant body by 2.45% with effect from 1st September 2008.

Increase of teaching and learning responsibility payments not yet in payment

24.1 This paragraph applies where the relevant body has conducted a review of their staffing structure and has determined that a TLR of a specified amount should attach to a particular post within the staff structure but the TLR is not yet in payment.

24.2 Subject to paragraph 22.2, the relevant body must increase the specified amount of the TLR by 2.45% with effect from 1st September 2008.

Safeguarding of teaching and learning responsibility payments

25.1 Subject to sub-paragraph 2, if the relevant body determines ("the determination"), whether as a result of a change to their pay policy or to the school's staffing structure, either–

(a) that the teacher's duties are no longer to include the significant responsibility for which the TLR was awarded; or

(b) that his significant responsibility (whether or not this has changed) merits, in accordance with their pay policy and staffing structure, a TLR of a lower annual value ("the new payment"),

it must pay him the safeguarded sum.

25.2 TLRs awarded to teachers employed under a fixed-term contract or whilst they occupy another post in the temporary absence of the post-holder must not be safeguarded after the fixed-term contract expires or after the date or the circumstance (if occurring earlier than that date) notified to the teacher pursuant to paragraph 4.4(c)(iii) occurs.

25.3 The safeguarded sum in the case of a teacher referred to in–

(a) sub-paragraph 1(a) is the value of the TLR to which he was entitled immediately before the determination; and

(b) sub-paragraph 1(b) is the difference between the value of the TLR to which he was entitled immediately before the determination and the new payment.

25.4 Within one month of the date of the determination, the relevant body must notify the teacher in writing of–

(a) the reason for the determination;

(b) the date on which the teacher's TLR ends and, if applicable, from which the new payment comes into effect;

(c) the value immediately before the determination of the point at which he is placed on the pay scale set out either in paragraph 17.3 or in paragraph 19.2, taking into account the annual determination required by paragraph 4.1 ("the original salary");

(d) the safeguarded sum;

(e) (i) the date on which the safeguarding period will end (determined in accordance with paragraph 5.3);

(ii) where the safeguarded sum is paid in respect of a TLR awarded to a teacher employed under a fixed-term contract, the date on which that fixed-term contract and payment of the safeguarded sum will end; or

(iii) where the safeguarded sum is paid in respect of a TLR awarded to a teacher whilst he occupies another post in the temporary absence of the post-holder, the date or the circumstance (if occurring earlier than that date) notified to the teacher pursuant to paragraph 4.4(c)(iii) on which the award and payment of the safeguarded sum will end; and

(f) where a copy of the school's staffing structure and pay policy may be inspected.

25.5 Subject to paragraphs 5.1, 5.2 and sub-paragraphs 6 and 7, the teacher must be paid the safeguarded sum until–

(a) (i) the safeguarding period ends;

(ii) where the safeguarded sum is paid in respect of a TLR awarded to a teacher employed under a fixed-term contract, the date on which that fixed-term contract expires; or

(iii) where the safeguarded sum is paid in respect of a TLR awarded to a teacher whilst he occupies another post in the temporary absence of the post-holder, the date or the circumstance (if occurring earlier than that date) notified to the teacher pursuant to paragraph 4.4(c)(iii) occurs;

(b) the teacher ceases to be a classroom teacher;

(c) the teacher is awarded a TLR as a result of a subsequent determination by the relevant body that equals or exceeds the combined value of the new payment (if any) and the safeguarded sum;

(d) the teacher is placed on a higher point on the pay scale set out either in paragraph 17.3 or in paragraph 19.2, or he first becomes entitled to be paid on the pay scale set out in paragraph 19.2 as a result of a subsequent determination; and the combined value of that point and any new payment equals or exceeds the combined value of his original salary and the safeguarded sum; or

(e) the teacher's employment at the school ends other than in circumstances to which paragraph 45 or 46 applies,

whichever is the first to occur.

25.6 The safeguarded sum must be reduced by the value of any subsequent TLR awarded to the teacher by the relevant body from time to time and in the case where the subsequent TLR is awarded to a teacher whilst he occupies another post in the temporary absence of the post-holder, restored upon the expiry of the period of that award, unless, in the meantime, any of the events specified in sub-paragraph 5 occurs.

25.7 Payment of the safeguarded sum must be discontinued whilst the teacher occupies a post as a member of the leadership group, as an advanced skills teacher or as an excellent teacher in the temporary absence of the post-holder but reinstated thereafter, unless, in the meantime, any of the events specified in sub-paragraph 5 occurs.

Special educational needs allowance

26.1 The annual value of a first SEN allowance is £1,912, and the annual value of a second SEN allowance is £3,778.

26.2 The relevant body must award a first SEN allowance to a classroom teacher-

(a) in a special school; or

(b) in an ordinary school who is engaged wholly or mainly-

(i) in teaching pupils with statements of special educational needs in designated special classes; or

(ii) in taking charge of special classes consisting wholly or mainly of children who are hearing impaired or visually impaired.

26.3 The relevant body may award a first SEN allowance to a classroom teacher in an ordinary school.

26.4 A SEN allowance may be awarded under sub-paragraph 3 only where the relevant body considers that the classroom teacher makes a particular contribution to the teaching of pupils with special educational needs in the school which is significantly greater than that which would normally be expected of a classroom teacher.

26.5 The relevant body may award a second SEN allowance to a classroom teacher who would otherwise be entitled to, or eligible for, a first SEN allowance and who has experience or qualifications or both which the relevant body considers are particularly relevant to the teacher's work.

Assimilation safeguarding

27.1 Subject to paragraphs 5.1, 5.2 and sub-paragraph 2, a classroom teacher who on 31st December 2005 was entitled to any sum under paragraph 28 of the 2000 Document, to the extent that paragraph 29([64]) of that Document provides for the continuing payment of that sum ("the safeguarded sum") after 1st January 2006, must be paid the safeguarded sum until–

(64) Paragraph 29 of the 2000 Document was amended by S.I. 2001/1254.

(a) 31st December 2008;

(b) he ceases to be a classroom teacher;

(c) he is placed on a higher point on the pay scale set out either in paragraph 17.3 or in paragraph 19.2, or he first becomes entitled to be paid on the pay scale in paragraph 19.2; and the value of that point equals or exceeds the combined value of the point to which he was entitled on 31st December 2005 and the safeguarded sum; or

(d) his employment at the school ends other than in circumstances to which paragraph 45 or 46 applies,

whichever is the first to occur.

27.2 Payment of the safeguarded sum must be discontinued whilst the teacher occupies a post as a member of the leadership group, as an advanced skills teacher or as an excellent teacher in the temporary absence of the post-holder but reinstated thereafter, unless, in the meantime, any of the events specified in sub-paragraph 1 occurs.

Second or subsequent appointment

28.1 A classroom teacher taking up an appointment on or after 1st September 2008, which is his second or subsequent one as such (whether or not after a break in service and whether on a full-time, part-time, regular, day to day or short term basis), who has not previously been placed on the pay scale for classroom teachers in accordance with any of the Documents published between 2002 and 2007, must be placed on a point determined in accordance with sub-paragraphs 2 and 3.

28.2.1 Subject to sub-paragraph 3, if he was last paid as a qualified teacher under the provisions of any of the Documents published between 1993 and 2001, he is entitled to-

(a) the equivalent point on the pay scale set out in paragraph 17.3, ascertained in accordance with the following table;

1993 to 1998 Documents and 1999 Document before its amendment by S.I.2000/868 (1st September 1999 to 31st March 2000)- minimum number of points	1999 Document after its amendment by S.I. 2000/868 (1st April 2000 to 31st August 2000)- minimum number of points	Point on pay scales in 2000 and 2001 Documents- Point on pay scale in paragraph 17.3 of 2000 Document, 15.3 of 2001 Document	Scale point on pay scale to which teacher assimilates
0	0	1	M1
1	0	1	M1
2	1	2	M1
3	2	3	M2
4	3	4	M3
5	4	5	M3
6	5	6	M4
7	6	7	M5
8	7	8	M6
9	8	9	M6

(b) one point in respect of each year of employment (interpreted in accordance with paragraph 1.8) as a classroom teacher completed since he was last placed on a point in accordance with the provisions of any such Document; and,

(c) at the relevant body's discretion, 1 or more points for years of experience other than employment as a classroom teacher which the relevant body considers to be of value to the classroom teacher's duties.

28.2.2 If he was last paid as a qualified teacher under the provisions of a pre-1993 document, the relevant body must determine the equivalent point.

28.3 A classroom teacher who-

(a) at any time on or after 1st September 2000 and prior to his employment as a classroom teacher was employed as a head teacher, deputy head teacher or assistant head teacher;

(b) was first appointed to a post of head teacher, deputy head teacher or assistant head teacher on or after 1st September 2000; and

(c) occupied a post or posts of head teacher, deputy head teacher or assistant head teacher for an aggregate period of less than one year,

must not be placed at less than point M6 on the pay scale set out in paragraph 17.3.

28.4 A post-threshold teacher taking up an appointment which is his second or subsequent one as a teacher (whether or not after a break in service and whether on a full-time, part-time, regular, day to day or short term basis), must be paid a salary determined in accordance with paragraph 19.

Advanced Skills Teachers

Pay spine for advanced skills teachers

29.1 An advanced skills teacher must be paid such salary based on the following pay spine as the relevant body determines in accordance with sub-paragraphs 2 to 8.

Pay Spine for Advanced Skills Teachers

Spine point	Annual Salary England and Wales (excluding the London Area)	Annual Salary Inner London Area	Annual Salary Outer London Area	Annual Salary Fringe Area
	£	£	£	£
AST 1	35,794	42,559	38,634	36,781
AST 2	36,692	43,460	39,532	37,679
AST 3	37,608	44,379	40,445	38,594
AST 4	38,545	45,313	41,388	39,535
AST 5	39,504	46,278	42,347	40,497
AST 6	40,494	47,265	43,334	41,484
AST 7	41,585	48,359	44,428	42,578
AST 8	42,544	49,315	45,387	43,530
AST 9	43,607	50,375	46,447	44,597
AST 10	44,726	51,497	47,569	45,716
AST 11	45,888	52,653	48,725	46,874

Pay Spine for Advanced Skills Teachers

Spine point	Annual Salary England and Wales (excluding the London Area)	Annual Salary Inner London Area	Annual Salary Outer London Area	Annual Salary Fringe Area
	£	£	£	£
AST 12	46,945	53,716	49,788	47,938
AST 13	48,119	54,890	50,962	49,112
AST 14	49,318	56,089	52,155	50,308
AST 15	50,547	57,312	53,384	51,531
AST 16	51,890	58,661	54,730	52,880
AST 17	53,083	59,854	55,923	54,079
AST 18	54,417	61,188	57,260	55,406

SECTION 2

29.2 Subject to sub-paragraph 4, a relevant body which appoints an advanced skills teacher must determine a pay range consisting of five consecutive points on the pay spine set out in sub-paragraph 1 for that teacher and the point in that range on which the advanced skills teacher must be paid.

29.3 When determining an appropriate five point pay range, the relevant body must have regard in particular (but not exclusively) to the following criteria-

(a) the nature of the work to be undertaken, including any work with teachers from other schools;

(b) the degree of challenge of the role;

(c) the professional competencies required of the teacher; and

(d) such other criteria as they consider appropriate.

29.4 Where a person is appointed as an advanced skills teacher for the first time he must be placed on the lowest point on his pay range.

29.5 Where the teacher is not subject to the 2002 Regulations or the 2006 Regulations, the relevant body must annually agree performance criteria with the advanced skills teacher and review performance against those criteria.

29.6 When making the annual determination of the salary of an advanced skills teacher, the relevant body must not determine that there be any movement up the pay spine unless-

(a) in the case where the advanced skills teacher is not subject to the 2002 Regulations or the 2006 Regulations, there has been a sustained high quality of performance by him, having regard to-

(i) the performance criteria previously agreed between the relevant body and the teacher; and

(ii) any work the teacher has carried out with or for the benefit of teachers from other schools; or

(b) where the advanced skills teacher is subject to the 2002 Regulations or the 2006 Regulations, there has been a sustained high quality of performance by him, having regard to the results of the most recent appraisal carried out in accordance with the 2002 Regulations or the results of the most recent review carried out in accordance with the 2006 Regulations, as the case may be,

and any such movement must not exceed two spine points in the course of one school year.

29.7 When making any determination in accordance with sub-paragraph 6 in the case of an advanced skills teacher who is subject to the 2006 Regulations, the relevant body must have regard to any recommendation on pay progression recorded in the teacher's most recent planning and review statement.

29.8 Where the relevant body raises the pay range for an advanced skills teacher, any performance points awarded by the relevant body for the previous year must be calculated on the basis of the lower pay range before the advanced skills teacher's pay is assimilated onto the higher pay range.

Assessment against the advanced skills teacher standards and the excellent teacher standards

Eligibility

30.1 A classroom teacher who is not a post-threshold teacher who has been selected for interview for an advanced skills teacher post is eligible to apply for assessment against the post-threshold teacher standards, the excellent teacher standards and the advanced skills teacher standards.

30.2 A post-threshold teacher who has been selected for interview for an advanced skills teacher post is eligible to apply for assessment against the excellent teacher standards and the advanced skills teacher standards.

30.3 An excellent teacher who has been selected for interview for an advanced skills teacher post is eligible to apply for assessment against the advanced skills teacher standards.

30.4 A post-threshold teacher who is placed at point U3 on the pay scale set out in paragraph 19.2 and who is employed by a relevant body that has an excellent teacher's post that is vacant, is eligible to apply for assessment against the excellent teacher standards.

Appointment of assessors

31.1 The Secretary of State must make arrangements for the appointment of assessors for the purposes of paragraph 33.

31.2 The arrangements must include arrangements for the quality of assessments to be monitored and for the independent review of assessments.

31.3 An assessor appointed under this paragraph must exercise his functions without unlawful discrimination.

Advanced skills teacher and excellent teacher pre-assessment

32.1 Sub-paragraphs 1 to 7 apply where an eligible teacher ("the applicant") applies for assessment against the relevant standards set out in Annex 1.

32.2 Before he can be assessed against the relevant standards by an assessor, the applicant must meet the standards which apply to any person on the same pay scale or pay spine as the applicant or, where the applicant is an excellent teacher, any person on an excellent teacher's salary.

32.3 Except where the applicant is an unattached teacher, the relevant body must delegate the task of determining whether an applicant meets the standards referred to in sub-paragraph 2 to the head teacher.

32.4 Where the applicant is an unattached teacher, the relevant body must delegate the task of determining whether the applicant meets the standards referred to in sub-paragraph 2 to a person with management responsibility for the applicant.

32.5 When determining whether an applicant meets the standards referred to in sub-paragraph 2 in the case where the applicant is subject to the 2002 Regulations or the 2006 Regulations, the person to whom the task has been delegated must have regard to the results of the teacher's most recent appraisal carried out in accordance with the 2002 Regulations or the most recent review carried out in accordance with the 2006 Regulations, as the case may be.

32.6 Where the person to whom the task of determining whether the applicant meets the standards referred to in sub-paragraph 2 has been delegated is not satisfied that the applicant meets those standards, he must reject the application and inform the applicant, giving reasons.

32.7 Where the person to whom the task of determining whether the applicant meets the standards referred to in sub-paragraph 2 has been delegated is satisfied that the applicant meets those standards, he must inform the applicant and pass the application, together with all the evidence, to the assessor.

Advanced skills teacher and excellent teacher assessment

33.1 Sub-paragraphs 2 to 4 apply where an eligible teacher ("the applicant") applies for assessment against the relevant standards set out in Annex 1.

33.2 The assessor must assess the applicant against the relevant standards and determine whether he meets them.

33.3 The assessor must inform the applicant of his decision, and where he determines that the applicant does not meet the relevant standards, give reasons.

33.4 Where the assessor determines that the applicant meets the relevant standards, he must also issue a certificate to that effect.

Review of assessment

34.1 An applicant who is assessed as not meeting the relevant standards is entitled to apply for an independent review of the assessment upon the grounds set out in sub-paragraph 2 (but no other grounds).

34.2 The grounds for review are that the applicant would have been assessed as meeting the relevant standards if-

(a) proper account had been taken of relevant evidence;

(b) account had not been taken of irrelevant or inaccurate evidence;

(c) the assessment had not been biased; or

(d) the assessment had not been conducted in a manner that unlawfully discriminated against the applicant.

34.3 The person conducting the review must take such steps as he thinks fit.

34.4 Where the outcome of the review is a determination that, on one or more of the grounds set out in sub-paragraph 2, the applicant should have been assessed as meeting the relevant standards set out in Annex 1, the person conducting the review must issue a certificate stating that the applicant meets the standards.

Excellent teachers and chartered London teachers

Excellent teachers – Eligibility for appointment

35.1 A teacher may be appointed to an excellent teacher post if he-

(a) has held an excellent teacher post; or

(b) is a post-threshold teacher who has completed at least two years of employment (interpreted in accordance with

SECTION 2

paragraph 1.8) since he was first placed at point U3 on the pay scale set out in paragraph 19.2 or the equivalent pay scale in an earlier Document and-

(i) in accordance with the 2004 Document or any previous Document, has been assessed as meeting the standards for advanced skills teachers applicable at the relevant time; or

(ii) has been certified by an assessor as meeting the standards set out in Annex 2 of the 2005 Document or of the 2006 Document; or

(iii) in accordance with this Document or the 2007 Document, has satisfied the person to whom the task has been delegated that he meets the core standards and the post-threshold standards and been certified by an assessor as meeting the excellent teacher standards or the advanced skills teacher standards.

Determination of salary

35.2 The salary of any person appointed as an excellent teacher on or after 1st September 2008 must be determined in accordance with sub-paragraphs 4 and 5.

35.3 The salary of existing excellent teachers must be re-determined by the relevant body with effect from 1st September 2008 in accordance with sub-paragraphs 4 and 5.

35.4 Where an excellent teacher is employed in inner London his salary must be no less than £37,672 and no more than £53,819 and where an excellent teacher is employed elsewhere his salary must be no less than £37,672 and no more than £48,437.

35.5 When determining the salary for an excellent teacher within the range referred to in sub-paragraph 4 the relevant body must have regard only to-

(a) the nature of the work to be undertaken; and

(b) the degree of challenge of the role.

35.6 The relevant body may re-determine the salary of an excellent teacher at any time where there are any significant changes in-

(a) the nature of the work to be undertaken; or

(b) the degree of challenge of the role.

Safeguarding

35.7 Where the salary of an excellent teacher is reduced following a re-determination under sub-paragraph 3 or 6, the teacher must be paid the safeguarded sum.

35.8 The safeguarded sum is the difference between the value of the salary to which the teacher was entitled immediately before the determination ("original salary") and the value of the new salary.

35.9 Within one month of any determination to reduce the salary of an excellent teacher under sub-paragraph 3 or sub-paragraph 6, the relevant body must notify the excellent teacher in writing of that fact and of-

(a) the reason for the determination;

(b) the teacher's original salary;

(c) the safeguarded sum;

(d) (i) in the case where the salary is reduced under sub-paragraph 3, the date on which the safeguarded sum will cease to be payable (31st August 2011);

(ii) in the case where the salary is reduced under sub-paragraph 6, the date on which the safeguarding period will end, determined in accordance with paragraph 5.3; or

(iii) in the case of a teacher employed as an excellent teacher for a fixed period or under a fixed-term contract, the date or the circumstance the occurrence of which will bring that fixed period or fixed-term contract to an end.

SECTION 2

35.10 Payment of the safeguarded sum must be discontinued whilst the teacher occupies a post as a member of the leadership group or as an advanced skills teacher in the temporary absence of the post-holder but restored thereafter, unless, in the meantime, any of the events referred to in sub-paragraph 11 occurs.

35.11 Subject to paragraph 5.1, the safeguarded sum must be paid to the excellent teacher until-

(a) (i) in the case where the salary is reduced under sub-paragraph 3, 31st August 2011; or

(ii) in the case where the salary is reduced under sub-paragraph 6, the safeguarding period ends;

(b) in the case where a teacher is employed as an excellent teacher for a fixed period or under a fixed-term contract, the date on which that fixed period or fixed-term contract expires;

(c) his salary is increased following a further review under sub-paragraph 6 and the increase in salary exceeds the safeguarded sum;

(d) he ceases to be an excellent teacher; or

(e) his employment at the school ends, other than in circumstances to which paragraph 45 or 46 applies;

whichever is the first to occur.

Chartered London teachers

36.1 A qualified teacher who intends to apply for chartered London teacher status must register his intention to do so with the Secretary of State or with such person or body as may be appointed by the Secretary of State for that purpose.

36.2 A teacher cannot so register unless at the time of registration he is employed by an authority or a governing body in the Inner or Outer London Area.

36.3 A qualified teacher who has so registered (whether under this Document or an earlier Document) may apply once in a school year to the relevant body for chartered London teacher status if he satisfies the requirements in sub-paragraph 4.

36.4 The requirements are that, at the date of the application–

(a) he has completed not less than four years of employment (interpreted in accordance with paragraph 1.8), in a head of teaching or teaching role in an academy, city technology college, city college for the technology of the arts, a non-maintained special school or a school in the Inner or Outer London Area and is currently employed as a teacher with an authority or a governing body in the Inner or Outer London Area;

(b) two years have elapsed since he registered his intention to apply; and

(c) he is a post-threshold teacher, an advanced skills teacher, an excellent teacher or a member of the leadership group.

36.5 Where an applicant is employed to teach at more than one school he may not apply to the relevant body of more than one such school.

36.6 Except where the applicant is an unattached teacher or is the head teacher, the relevant body must delegate the receipt and assessment of the application to the head teacher.

36.7 Where the applicant is an unattached teacher, the relevant body must delegate the receipt and assessment of the application to a person with management responsibility for the applicant.

36.8 The applicant must be assessed against the standards set out in Annex 2 and if it is determined that the applicant met all the standards during the period between registering his intention to apply and his application the relevant body must award the applicant chartered London teacher status.

36.9 A chartered London teacher must be paid the sum of £1000 in the school year in which he is awarded chartered London teacher status.

PART 5 – Unqualified Teachers

SECTION 2

Pay scale for unqualified teachers

37.1 Each unqualified teacher must be paid such salary as the relevant body determines in accordance with the provisions of this paragraph and paragraph 38.

37.2 The previous pay scale for unqualified teachers is:

Pay Scale for Unqualified Teachers until 31st August 2008

Scale point	Annual Salary England and Wales (excluding the London Area)	Annual Salary Inner London Area	Annual Salary Outer London Area	Annual Salary Fringe Area
	£	£	£	£
1	14,751	18,552	17,523	15,720
2	15,417	19,215	18,186	16,383
3	16,056	19,857	18,831	17,028
4	16,722	20,523	19,497	17,694
5	17,397	21,201	20,169	18,366
6	18,045	21,846	20,820	19,011
7	18,711	22,509	21,483	19,674
8	20,256	24,054	23,031	21,225
9	22,011	25,809	24,786	22,977
10	23,331	27,129	26,106	24,297

37.3 The new pay scale for unqualified teachers is:

Pay Scale for Unqualified Teachers from 1st September 2008

Scale point	Annual Salary England and Wales (excluding the London Area)	Annual Salary Inner London Area	Annual Salary Outer London Area	Annual Salary Fringe Area
	£	£	£	£
1	15,113	19,007	17,953	16,106
2	16,871	20,764	19,711	17,863
3	18,629	22,522	21,470	19,620
4	20,387	24,279	23,229	21,378
5	22,145	26,037	24,987	23,135
6	23,903	27,794	26,746	24,893

37.4 The assimilation table for unqualified teachers is:

Assimilation Table for Unqualified Teachers

Scale point on previous pay scale on which teacher is placed	Scale point on new pay scale to which teacher is assimilated
1	1
2	2
3	2
4	3
5	3
6	3
7	4
8	5
9	6
10	6

Teachers in post prior to 1st September 2008

37.5 In the case of an unqualified teacher who was employed as such on 31st August 2008 or at any time before that date, the relevant body must determine the point above point 1 on the previous pay scale on which that teacher is to be placed in accordance with sub-paragraph 6; and if an unqualified teacher is not entitled to any points under that sub-paragraph he must be placed at point 1 on that pay scale.

37.6 For the purposes of sub-paragraph 5, a teacher must be placed at that point on the pay scale which is equal to the total number of points awarded to the teacher-

(a) in accordance with sub-paragraphs 8 and 10; and

(b) if applicable, in accordance with sub-paragraph 11.

37.7 After determining the point on the previous pay scale on which the unqualified teacher is to be placed in accordance with sub-paragraphs 5 and 6, the relevant body must determine the point on the new pay scale on which the unqualified teacher is to be placed in accordance with the assimilation table.

SECTION 2

Mandatory points

37.8 When determining where to place a teacher on the previous pay scale under sub-paragraph 5, the relevant body must award-

(a) if applicable, the number of points awarded in accordance with the 2005 Document, the 2006 Document or the 2007 Document, whichever of these was the latest Document under which the teacher was awarded any such points;

(b) if applicable and subject to sub-paragraph 9, 1 point for the year of employment (interpreted in accordance with paragraph 1.8) completed as an unqualified teacher since his salary was last determined in accordance with the 2005 Document, the 2006 Document or the 2007 Document, as the case may be.

37.9 A year of employment is not to be counted for the purposes of sub-paragraph 8(b) where the teacher has been notified in accordance with the 2005 Document, the 2006 Document, the 2007 Document or sub-paragraph 10.3 below, as the case may be, that his service was unsatisfactory in respect of that year.

37.10.1 Where an unqualified teacher remains in service on 1st September in the school in which he was employed during the previous school year, the relevant body must decide for the purposes of sub-paragraph 8(b) whether or not his service has been satisfactory.

37.10.2 Before reaching a decision under sub-paragraph 10.1 the relevant body must seek and take into account advice from the head teacher of the school.

37.10.3 Where the relevant body decides under sub-paragraph 10.1 that an unqualified teacher's service has been unsatisfactory, it must notify the teacher in writing of that fact before the end of the current school year and before the relevant body makes a determination for the purposes of sub-paragraph 5.

Discretionary points

37.11 When determining where to place a teacher on the previous pay scale under sub-paragraph 5 the relevant body may also award-

(a) 1 point to an unqualified teacher who has been notified that a year of employment has not been satisfactory in respect of that year;

(b) 1 or more points for years of experience other than employment as an unqualified teacher which the relevant body considers to be of value to the performance of the unqualified teacher's duties;

(c) in a case to which paragraph 4.1(a) applies, 1 point-

(i) where the teacher is not subject to the 2002 Regulations or the 2006 Regulations, his performance in the previous school year was excellent, having regard to all aspects of his professional duties, in particular, classroom teaching; or

(ii) where the teacher is subject to the 2002 Regulations or the 2006 Regulations, his performance in the previous school year was excellent, having regard to the results of the most recent appraisal carried out in accordance with the 2002 Regulations or the most recent review carried out in accordance with the 2006 Regulations, as the case may be;

(d) in the case of a teacher who was not employed as an unqualified teacher between 1st September 2005 and 31st August 2008, 1 point for each year of employment completed as an unqualified teacher prior to 1st September 2005.

37.12 When making any determination in accordance with sub-paragraph 11(c)(ii) in the case of an unqualified teacher who is subject to the 2006 Regulations, the relevant body must have regard to any recommendation on pay progression recorded in the teacher's most recent planning and review statement.

New teachers

37.13 Subject to sub-paragraph 14, where a person is appointed for the first time with effect from 1st September 2008 or thereafter the relevant body must place him on point 1 of the new pay scale.

37.14 Where the person referred to in sub-paragraph 13 has experience other than employment as an unqualified teacher which the relevant body considers to be of value to the performance of the unqualified teacher's duties, the relevant body may place him on a point above point 1 on the new pay scale, in which case it must determine the point above point 1 which is appropriate for that teacher in the light of that experience.

SECTION 2

General

37.15 Any points awarded under this paragraph are permanent whether the unqualified teacher remains in the same post or takes up a new one.

Allowance payable to unqualified teachers

38.1 The relevant body may determine that such additional allowance as it considers appropriate is to be paid to an unqualified teacher where it considers, in the context of its staffing structure and pay policy, that the teacher has-

(a) taken on a sustained additional responsibility which is-

(i) focused on teaching and learning; and

(ii) requires the exercise of a teachers' professional skills and judgment; or

(b) qualifications or experience which bring added value to the role he is undertaking.

38.2 Where an unqualified teacher is in receipt of an additional allowance awarded under a previous Document, the relevant body must re-determine that allowance in accordance with the criteria specified in sub-paragraph 1 with effect from 1st September 2008.

Safeguarding

38.3 Where the relevant body determines, in respect of a teacher who is in receipt of an allowance, whether as a result of a change to its pay policy or to the school's staffing structure, that–

(a) the teacher's duties are no longer to include the additional responsibility in respect of which the allowance was awarded and, therefore, that the allowance should be withdrawn;

(b) the additional responsibility in respect of which the allowance was awarded now merits the payment of a lower allowance ("the new allowance"); or

(c) the teacher's duties are no longer to include the additional responsibility in respect of which the allowance was awarded but are to include a different additional responsibility which merits the payment of a lower allowance ("the new allowance"),

it must pay the teacher the safeguarded sum.

38.4 Where the re-determination referred to in sub-paragraph 2 leads to-

(a) a withdrawal of the allowance; or

(b) a lower allowance,

the relevant body must pay the teacher the safeguarded sum.

38.5 The safeguarded sum in the case of any teacher referred to in–

(a) sub-paragraph 3(a) or sub-paragraph 4(a) is the value of the allowance to which the teacher was entitled immediately before the determination was made to withdraw it;

(b) sub-paragraph 3(b) or (c) or sub-paragraph 4(b)is the difference between the value of the allowance to which the teacher was entitled immediately before the determination was made to lower the allowance and the value of the new allowance.

38.6 The safeguarded sum must be reduced by the value of any subsequent allowance awarded to the teacher by the relevant body from time to time and, in the case where the subsequent allowance is awarded whilst the teacher occupies another post in the temporary absence of the post-holder, restored upon the expiry of the period of that allowance, unless, in the meantime, any of the events specified in sub-paragraph 9 occurs.

38.7 Where a safeguarded sum is payable under sub-paragraph 3, the relevant body must notify the teacher in writing, within one month of the date of the determination, of-

(a) the reason for the determination;

(b) the safeguarded sum;

(c) the date on which the teacher's allowance is to be withdrawn altogether or replaced with a new lower allowance, as the case may be;

(d) where the old allowance was awarded for a fixed period, the date the fixed period expires;

(e) where the old allowance was awarded to a teacher employed under a fixed-term contract, the date on which that fixed-term contract expires;

(f) the date on which the safeguarding period will end (determined in accordance with paragraph 5.3);

(g) taking into account the annual determination required by paragraph 4.1, the value of the salary immediately before the determination of the point at which he is placed on the new pay scale in accordance with paragraph 37.7 ("the original salary"); and

(h) the details of where a copy of the school's staffing structure and pay policy may be inspected.

38.8 Where a safeguarded sum is payable under sub-paragraph 4, the relevant body must notify the teacher in writing, on or before 30th September 2008, of–

(a) the information specified in sub-paragraph 7(a) to (d);

(b) taking into account the annual determination required by paragraph 4.1, the value of the salary immediately before the determination of the point at which he is placed on the new pay scale in accordance with paragraph 37.7 ("the original salary").

38.9 Subject to paragraph 5.1 and 5.2, the teacher must be paid the safeguarded sum until–

(a) (i) in the case of a teacher who is paid the safeguarded sum under sub-paragraph 3, the date on which the safeguarding period ends; or

(ii) in the case of a teacher who is paid the safeguarded sum under sub-paragraph 4, 31st August 2011;

(b) where the allowance was awarded for a fixed period, the date on which the fixed period expires;

(c) where the allowance was awarded to a teacher employed under a fixed-term contract, the date on which that fixed-term contract expires;

(d) the date on which the teacher ceases to be an unqualified teacher;

(e) the date on which the teacher is awarded an allowance as a result of a subsequent determination by the relevant body that equals or exceeds the combined value of the new allowance (if any) and the safeguarded sum;

(f) the date on which the teacher is placed on a higher point on the pay scale set out in paragraph 37.3 and the combined value of that point and any new payment equals or exceeds the combined value of the teacher's original salary and the safeguarded sum; or

(g) the date on which the teacher's employment at the school ends, other than in circumstances to which paragraph 46 applies,

whichever is the first to occur.

38.10 In this paragraph any reference to an allowance is a reference to an allowance payable under this paragraph.

An unqualified teacher who becomes qualified

39.1 An unqualified teacher must be transferred to the next point on the classroom teachers' pay scale in paragraph 17.3 above the sum of his unqualified teacher's salary payable under paragraph 37 and any unqualified teachers' allowance payable under paragraph 38 (including any safeguarded sum payable under paragraph 38.4), or to such higher point on the classroom teachers' pay scale as the relevant body considers to be appropriate, upon obtaining qualified teacher status under regulations made under section 132 of the Act[65].

39.2 A teacher who obtains qualified teacher status retrospectively under those regulations must be paid a lump sum by the relevant body responsible for the payment of his remuneration at the time when his qualified teacher status was effectively obtained.

39.3 The lump sum payable under sub-paragraph 2 must be the difference (if any) between the remuneration he was actually paid as an unqualified teacher and the salary (not including any allowances) he would have been paid as a qualified teacher, from the date he effectively obtained qualified teacher status to the date when the lump sum is paid.

(65) S.I. 2003/1662 in relation to England and S.I. 2004/1729 (W173) in relation to Wales.

PART 6 – Additional Allowances

SECTION 2

Social priority allowance and Inner London Area supplement

40.1 Subject to paragraphs 5.1 and 5.2 and sub-paragraph 2, a teacher who was entitled to an allowance under paragraph 17 of the 1988 Document or under sub-paragraph (5) or (6) of paragraph 18 of the 1993 Document on 31st December 2005 must be paid that allowance ("the safeguarded sum") until-

(a) 31st December 2008;

(b) the teacher is placed on a point on a different pay scale or pay spine, or takes up an excellent teacher post, but this does not apply to a classroom teacher when he is first placed on the pay scale set out in paragraph 19.2 or to a teacher affected by a determination made by a relevant body under paragraph 47;

(c) the teacher is placed on a higher point on the applicable pay scale or pay spine, and the value of that point equals or exceeds the combined value of the point to which he was entitled on 31st December 2005 and the safeguarded sum; or

(d) the teacher's employment at the school ends other than in circumstances to which paragraph 45 or 46 applies,

whichever is the first to occur.

40.2 Payment of the safeguarded sum must be discontinued whilst the teacher occupies a post as a member of the leadership group, as an advanced skills teacher or as an excellent teacher in the temporary absence of the post-holder but reinstated thereafter, unless, in the meantime, any of the events specified in sub-paragraph 1 occurs.

Acting allowance

41.1 Subject to sub-paragraph 7, where a teacher is assigned and carries out duties of a head teacher, deputy head teacher or assistant head teacher, but has not been appointed as an acting head teacher, deputy head teacher or assistant head teacher, the relevant body must, within the period of four weeks beginning on the day on which he is first assigned and carries out duties of a head teacher, deputy head teacher or assistant head teacher, determine whether or not he must be paid an allowance in accordance with the following provisions ("acting allowance").

41.2 If the relevant body's determination referred to in sub-paragraph 1 is that the teacher must not be paid an acting allowance, but the teacher continues to be assigned and to carry out duties of a head teacher, deputy head teacher or assistant head teacher (and has not been appointed as an acting head teacher, deputy head teacher or assistant head teacher), the relevant body may at any time after that determination make a further determination as to whether or not he must be paid an acting allowance.

41.3 If the relevant body determines that the teacher must be paid an acting allowance, subject to sub-paragraph 4, it must be of such amount as is necessary to ensure that he receives remuneration equivalent to such point on the leadership group pay spine set out in paragraph 6.4 as the relevant body considers to be appropriate.

41.4 The remuneration of a teacher who is assigned and carries out duties of a head teacher must not be lower than the minimum of the individual school range, and where a teacher is assigned and carries out the duties of a deputy or assistant head teacher in relation to whom a deputy or assistant head teacher pay range (as the case may be) has been determined, his remuneration must not be lower than the minimum of that range.

41.5 The teacher may be paid an acting allowance with effect from such day on or after the day on which he is first assigned and carries out duties of a head teacher, deputy head teacher or assistant head teacher as the relevant body may determine.

41.6 Where a teacher is paid an allowance under this paragraph, then for so long as he is paid that allowance-

(a) where he is assigned and carries out duties of a head teacher, Part 9 applies to him as if he had been appointed to the post of head teacher and Parts 10, 11 and 12 do not apply to him;

(b) where he is assigned and carries out the duties of a deputy head teacher or assistant head teacher, Parts 10 and 12 apply to him as if he had been appointed to the post of deputy head teacher or assistant head teacher and Part 11 does not apply to him.

Performance payments to seconded teachers

42. Where-

(a) a teacher is temporarily seconded to a post as head teacher in a school causing concern which is not his normal place of work; and

(b) the relevant body of that school considers that the teacher merits an additional point or points to reflect the sustained high quality of performance by him throughout the secondment,

that relevant body may pay the teacher a lump sum equal to the value of the additional point or points on that school's individual school range, if the teacher would otherwise not receive the full value of the point or points as a result of his return to his original school.

PART 7 – Supplementary

Determination of applicable pay scale

43.1 A teacher who is employed under a contract that normally requires him to work in the London Area but who is temporarily required to work elsewhere must continue to be paid in accordance with the pay scale applicable to his normal area of employment.

43.2 A teacher who on 31st August 2008 was being paid in accordance with one of the London Area pay scales must continue to be paid in accordance with that London Area pay scale notwithstanding that he would not otherwise be entitled to it under the provisions of this Document, for so long as he remains in the post that he held on that date.

43.3 A teacher who moves out of the Inner London Area may continue to be paid in accordance with the Inner London pay scale at the rate being paid before he moved for so long as he continues to be employed as a teacher in a post in which his salary is paid by the same authority.

43.4 A teacher who moves out of the Outer London Area, to anywhere but the Inner London Area, may continue to be paid on the Outer London Area scale at the rate being paid before he moved for so long as he continues to be employed as a teacher in a post in which his salary is paid by the same authority.

43.5 A teacher who moves out of the Fringe Area, to anywhere but the Inner London Area or the Outer London Area, may continue to be paid on the Fringe Area scale at the rate being paid before he moved for so long as he continues to be employed as a teacher in a post in which his salary is paid by the same authority.

43.6 In relation to a teacher holding an excellent teacher post the references in this paragraph to a pay scale or a pay spine are to be read as references to the teacher's salary determined in accordance with paragraph 35.2.

Unattached teachers

44.1 The remuneration of an unattached teacher must be determined in accordance with whichever provisions of this Document the relevant body considers to be appropriate in the circumstances of the case, having regard to its pay policy and the teacher's particular post within the staffing structure.

44.2 Where, in accordance with sub-paragraph 1, the remuneration of a teacher in charge of a pupil referral unit is determined in accordance with the provisions applicable to a head teacher, Part 9 applies to him and Part 12 does not apply to him.

44.3 Where, in accordance with sub-paragraph 1, the remuneration of an unattached teacher (other than a teacher in charge of a pupil referral unit) is determined in accordance with the provisions applicable to a member of the leadership group, Part 12 does not apply to him and his conditions of employment that relate to his professional duties and working time must be agreed between him and the relevant body.

44.4 Nothing in sub-paragraph 1 is to be taken to authorise an unattached teacher to whom paragraph 17.2 does not apply to be paid a salary based on the pay scale set out in paragraph 19.

44.5 Nothing in this paragraph is to be taken to authorise-

(a) paragraph 21 to be disapplied in the case of an unattached teacher; or

(b) an unattached teacher who is a post-threshold teacher to be paid a salary based on the pay scale set out in paragraph 17.3.

General safeguarding applicable to teachers taking up post on or before 31st December 2005

45.1 Subject to sub-paragraphs 4 to 9 of this paragraph-

45.1.1 where, as a result of-

(a) the closure or reorganisation of an educational establishment; or

(b) a direction relating to a course for the training of teachers given by the Secretary of State under regulation 3(2) of the Further Education Regulations 1975(66), under regulation 15 or 16 of the Education (Schools and Further Education) Regulations 1981(67) or under regulation 12 or 13 of the Education (Schools and Further and Higher Education) Regulations 1989(68),

(66) S.I. 1975/1054; revoked by S.I. 1984/74.
(67) S.I. 1981/1086; regulations 15 and 16 were revoked by S.I. 1999/3181.
(68) S.I. 1989/351.

a teacher (including a teacher in further or higher education) loses his post, and is on or before 31st December 2005 employed full-time as a teacher in the provision of primary or secondary education (whether or not at a school) in a post where his remuneration is paid by the same authority as before, he must be deemed for all salary purposes, including any assimilation onto a new pay scale or pay spine, to continue to hold the post he held, and to be entitled to those allowances listed in sub-paragraph 2 to which he was entitled immediately before the closure, reorganisation or direction;

45.1.2 where, in circumstances other than those mentioned in sub-paragraph 1.1, such a teacher loses his post and is on or before 31st December 2005 employed full-time as a teacher in the provision of primary or secondary education in a post (whether or not at a school) in which his remuneration is paid by the same authority as before he may, at the discretion of the authority be deemed for all salary purposes, including any assimilation onto a new pay scale or pay spine, to continue to hold the post he held, and to be entitled to those allowances listed in sub-paragraph 2 to which he was entitled immediately before the circumstances occurred; and the authority must not unreasonably refuse to exercise their discretion in this matter in favour of the teacher;

45.1.3 where in the circumstances described in sub-paragraphs 1.1 or 1.2 such a full-time teacher or such a teacher in regular part-time employment loses his post in circumstances described in sub-paragraph 1.1, and is thereupon employed as stated in that provision but as a teacher in regular part-time employment, he is (subject, in the circumstances described in sub-paragraph 1.2, to the same discretion to be similarly exercised) entitled to that proportion of the salary and of those allowances listed in sub-paragraph 2 to which he was entitled immediately before the relevant change in circumstances which his part-time employment bears to full-time employment.

45.2 The allowances referred to in sub-paragraphs 1.1 to 1.3 are-

(a) allowance for unqualified teachers (paragraph 38); and

(b) Inner London Area supplement and social priority allowance (paragraph 40) but only to the extent that paragraph provides for the continuing payment of those sums.

45.3 A teacher whose remuneration is safeguarded under this paragraph is entitled to an acting allowance (paragraph 41) only where appropriate to the circumstances of his present employment.

45.4 Subject to sub-paragraph 5, the salary to be safeguarded pursuant to sub-paragraph 1 means-

(a) any salary to which he is entitled under paragraph 17 or 19;

(b) any allowance to which he is entitled under paragraph 26; and

(c) any safeguarded sum to which he is entitled under paragraph 27, 47 and 48 but only to the extent that the applicable paragraph provides for the continuing payment of that sum.

45.5 For the purpose of the determination of a classroom teacher's entitlement under sub-paragraph 4-

(a) mandatory points awarded for experience under paragraph 18.1 must be re-assessed in accordance with paragraphs 4.1 and 42.1 until the maximum of the pay scale in paragraph 17.3 has been reached, and an amount based on such points must be included in the safeguarded salary;

(b) in relation to any management allowance awarded under any earlier document-

(i) paragraph 21 does not apply;

(ii) the allowance must be reduced by the value of any TLR awarded to the teacher by the relevant body from time to time and, in the case where the teacher is awarded a TLR whilst he occupies another post in the temporary absence of the post-holder, restored upon the expiry of the period of that award, unless, in the meantime, any of the events specified in sub-paragraph 8 occurs; and

(iii) an allowance awarded for a fixed period must only be included in the safeguarded salary for the period of that award;

(c) where the teacher becomes entitled to be paid as a post-threshold teacher his new salary and any subsequent progression on the pay scale in paragraph 19.2 must be included in his safeguarded salary; and

(d) where the teacher is, immediately before a circumstance mentioned in sub-paragraph 1.1 or 1.2 arises, entitled to be paid on the scale set out in paragraph 19.2 he remains so entitled and his salary on that scale including any subsequent progression must be included in his safeguarded salary.

45.6.1 Where a member of the leadership group is, immediately before a circumstance mentioned in sub-paragraph 1.1 or 1.2 arises, paid at a point on the leadership group pay spine pursuant to paragraph 6 he must continue (subject, in the circumstances mentioned in sub-paragraph 1.2 to the same discretion) to be paid at that point.

45.6.2 Where an advanced skills teacher is, immediately before a circumstance mentioned in sub-paragraph 1.1 or 1.2 arises, paid at a point on the advanced skills teacher pay spine pursuant to paragraph 29 he must continue (subject in the circumstances mentioned in sub-paragraph 1.2 to the same discretion) to be paid at that point.

45.7 If the teacher's safeguarded remuneration under this paragraph exceeds the remuneration to which he would otherwise be entitled under this Document by the sum of £500 or more, the relevant body must review the teacher's assigned duties and allocate such additional duties to him as it reasonably considers to be appropriate and commensurate with his safeguarded remuneration.

45.8 Sub-paragraph 1 does not apply or, as the case may be, ceases to apply, to a teacher-

(a) who at any time is offered but unreasonably refuses to accept an alternative post in an educational establishment maintained by the authority by which his salary is paid;

(b) if the remuneration payable to him by virtue of the other paragraphs of this Document equals or exceeds the remuneration payable under this paragraph;

(c) who is placed on a point on a different pay scale or pay spine or takes up an excellent teacher post, but this does not apply to a classroom teacher when he is first placed on the pay scale set out in paragraph 19.2 or to a teacher affected by a determination made by a relevant body under paragraph 47; or

(d) whose employment ends other than in circumstances to which this paragraph applies.

SECTION 2

45.9 For the purposes of this paragraph-

(a) "educational establishment" means an establishment in England and Wales which is-

(i) an institution of further or higher education maintained or assisted by an authority;

(ii) a school;

(iii) a teachers' centre; or

(iv) an establishment other than a school at which primary or secondary education is provided by an authority;

(b) "leadership group post" means a post of head teacher, deputy head teacher or assistant head teacher of a school;

(c) "remuneration" means salary plus any allowances but does not include any sum paid under paragraphs 51, 52 and 53;

(d) "salary" means-

(i) in the case of a school teacher, the salary payable in accordance with paragraphs 6, 17, 19, 29 and 37 including any allowance payable under paragraph 26, and

(ii) in the case of a teacher in further or higher education his basic salary excluding all allowances;

(e) a school is reorganised where it was or is reorganised in pursuance of proposals made under section 28 or 31 of the School Standards and Framework Act 1998(69) or proposals referred to in regulation 14 of the Education (Transition to New Framework) (School Organisation Proposals) Regulations 1999(70); and

(f) any transfer of the responsibility for maintaining an establishment must be disregarded.

(69) 1998 c.31 as amended by the Act.
(70) S.I. 1999/704.

General safeguarding applicable to teachers taking up post on or after 1st January 2006

46.1.1 This paragraph applies to a teacher who loses his post ("the old post"), as a result of-

(a) the discontinuance of a school;

(b) a prescribed alteration to, or the reorganisation of, a school; or

(c) the closure or reorganisation of any other educational establishment or service;

and who then takes up a new post on or after 1st January 2006 ("the new post") where he is employed by the same authority or at a school maintained by the same authority, and in the case of a teacher within Paragraph (b) the new post is at a different school.

46.1.2 In sub-paragraph 1.1 "prescribed alteration" means an alteration prescribed by the Education (School Organisation Proposals) (England) Regulations 1999(71) or the Education (School Organisation Proposals) (Wales) Regulations 1999(72).

SECTION 2

Re-determination of salary

46.2 The relevant body must determine in relation to the teacher-

(a) the pay scale, pay spine or salary point that applies to him in the new post and the appropriate point on that pay scale or pay spine on which the teacher should be placed, or the excellent teacher salary point, in accordance with the relevant paragraphs of this Document ("the new point"); and if, as a result, the teacher is placed on a point of lower value than that on which he was paid in the old post ("the old point"), the teacher must be paid in addition a sum equal to the difference in value between the old point and the new point ("the first safeguarded sum") as at the date of the implementation of the determination;

(b) any TLR that applies to the new post in accordance with paragraph 22; and the teacher is entitled to a safeguarded sum

(71) S.I. 1999/2213, amended by S.I. 2003/1229.
(72) S.I. 1999/1671, amended by S.I. 2004/908.

("the second safeguarded sum") in respect of the difference in value between that TLR and the value of any TLR of a higher value that was paid in relation to the old post or, if no TLR is awarded under this paragraph, in respect of the TLR that was paid in relation to the old post;

(c) any SEN allowance that applies to the new post in accordance with paragraph 26; and the teacher is entitled to a safeguarded sum ("the third safeguarded sum") in respect of the difference in value between that special educational needs allowance and the value of any SEN allowance of a higher value that was paid in relation to the old post or, if no SEN allowance is awarded under this paragraph, in respect of the SEN allowance that was paid in relation to the old post;

(d) in the case of an unqualified teacher, any allowance payable under paragraph 38 in relation to the new post; and the teacher is entitled to a safeguarded sum ("the fourth safeguarded sum") in respect of the difference in value between that allowance and the value of any such allowance of a higher value that was paid in relation to the old post or, if no allowance is awarded under this paragraph, in respect of the allowance that was paid in relation to the old post; and

(e) the value of any other allowances payable under this Document.

Reduction in the value of the safeguarded sums

46.3.1 The first safeguarded sum must be reduced by the value of any TLR or SEN allowance awarded to the teacher by the relevant body from time to time and, in the case where the teacher is awarded a TLR whilst he occupies another post in the temporary absence of the post-holder, restored upon the expiry of the period of that award, unless, in the meantime, any of the events specified in sub-paragraph 4 occurs.

46.3.2 If the relevant body subsequently awards the teacher a TLR or a TLR of higher value than the TLR awarded under sub-paragraph 2(b), the second safeguarded sum must be reduced by the value of the TLR or by a sum equal to the difference between the two TLRs, as the case may be.

46.3.3 If the relevant body subsequently awards the teacher a SEN allowance, or one of higher value than the SEN allowance awarded under sub-paragraph 2(c), the third safeguarded sum must be reduced by the value of the SEN allowance or by a sum equal to the difference between the two allowances, as the case may be.

46.3.4 If the relevant body subsequently awards the teacher an allowance under paragraph 38, or one of higher value than the allowance awarded under sub-paragraph 2(d), the fourth safeguarded sum must be reduced by the value of the allowance, or by a sum equal to the difference between the two allowances, as the case may be.

SECTION 2

The end of safeguarding

46.4 Subject to paragraph 5, the relevant body must pay the teacher the safeguarded sums to which he is entitled under sub-paragraph 2 until-

(a) the date on which the safeguarding period ends, being the third anniversary of the date on which the teacher starts work in the new post;

(b) the teacher is placed on a point on a different pay scale or pay spine, or takes up an excellent teacher post, but this does not apply to a classroom teacher when he is first placed on the pay scale set out in paragraph 19.2 or to a teacher affected by a determination made by a relevant body under paragraph 47;

(c) the teacher's employment ends other than in circumstances to which this paragraph applies; or

(d) the teacher is placed on a higher point on the applicable pay scale or pay spine, or is first placed on the pay scale set out in paragraph 19.2 and the value of that point equals or exceeds the combined value of the old point and any one or more of the safeguarded sums, in which case payment of those safeguarded sums must cease;

whichever is the first to occur.

Existing safeguarded sums preserved and R&R benefits safeguarded

46.5 Subject to paragraph 5.3, in addition to any sums to which the teacher is entitled under sub-paragraph 2, he must be paid-

(a) any safeguarded sums to which he continues to be entitled under paragraphs 21, 25, 27, 40, 47 and 48 until his entitlement ceases in circumstances set in those paragraphs; and

(b) any recruitment or retention incentive or benefit to which he was entitled under paragraph 53 in the old post, until either-

(i) the end of the fixed period for which it was awarded; or

(ii) the teacher accepts a different recruitment or retention incentive or benefit instead,

whichever is the first to occur.

Notification of determination

46.6 When notifying the teacher of its determination in accordance with paragraph 4.3, the relevant body must include details of the value of the pay point, allowances and all safeguarded sums to which the teacher was entitled in relation to the old post and to which he is entitled in relation to the new post, and in respect of safeguarded sums paid under this paragraph or under paragraphs 25, 35, 38, 47 and 48, of the date on which the safeguarding period ends.

Part-time teachers

46.7 Whether the teacher was a full-time teacher or a teacher in regular part-time employment before he lost his post, if he is then employed as stated in sub-paragraph 1.1 as a teacher in regular part-time employment, he must be paid a proportion of the remuneration to which he would have been entitled had he been employed as a full-time teacher, calculated in accordance with paragraph 49.

Safeguarding for members of the leadership group, advanced skills teachers and excellent teachers

47.1 Except where paragraph 48 applies and subject to paragraph 5, this paragraph applies where the relevant body determines ("the determination"), whether as a result of a change to its pay policy or to the school's staffing structure, to–

(a) reduce the number of members of the leadership group;

(b) end the designation of one or more advanced skills teachers' posts;

(c) end the designation of one or more excellent teachers' posts;

(d) lower the individual school range and this would lead to a reduction in the head teacher's salary;

(e) lower a deputy head teacher's pay range and this would lead to a reduction in the deputy head teacher's salary;

(f) lower an assistant head teacher's pay range and this would lead to a reduction in the assistant head teacher's salary;

(g) lower an advanced skills teacher's pay range and this would lead to a reduction in the advanced skills teacher's salary; or

(h) reduce an excellent teacher's salary.

47.2 A member of the leadership group, an advanced skills teacher or an excellent teacher whose salary is reduced as a result of the implementation of the determination must be paid the safeguarded sum.

47.3 In the case of a teacher who is affected by a determination within sub-paragraph 1(a) to (c), the safeguarded sum is the difference between his original salary (including the value of any performance points awarded by the relevant body for the previous year) and the value of the new point on which he is placed on the pay scale set out either in paragraph 17.3 or in paragraph 19.2 combined with any TLR or SEN allowance awarded to him.

47.4 In the case of a teacher who is affected by a determination within sub-paragraphs 1(d) to 1(h), the safeguarded sum is the difference

SECTION 2

between the original salary (including the value of any performance points awarded by the relevant body for the previous year) and the value of the point at which he is placed in the new pay range.

47.5 The relevant body must, within one month (and after having made the annual determination required by paragraph 4.1), notify in writing a teacher who is or may be affected by the determination of that fact and of–

(a) the reason for the determination;

(b) the date on which the determination is to be implemented in relation to that teacher (if known);

(c) the date on which the safeguarding period will end (determined in accordance with paragraph 5.3) or, in the case of a teacher employed as a member of the leadership group, as an advanced skills teacher or as an excellent teacher for a fixed period or under a fixed-term contract, the date or the circumstance the occurrence of which will bring that fixed period or fixed-term contract and payment of the safeguarded sum to an end;

(d) his original salary;

(e) the safeguarded sum or, if the determination is to be implemented at a later date and its precise effect on the teacher is not yet known, the maximum amount by which his original point may be reduced; and

(f) where a copy of the school's staffing structure and pay policy may be inspected.

47.6 Subject to paragraphs 5.1 and 5.2 and sub-paragraph 7, the teacher must be paid the safeguarded sum until–

(a) the safeguarding period ends or in the case of a teacher employed as a member of the leadership group, as an advanced skills teacher or as an excellent teacher for a fixed period or under a fixed-term contract, the date on which that fixed period or fixed-term contract ends;

(b) in the case of a teacher affected by a determination within sub-paragraphs 1(a) to 1(c)–

(i) he ceases to be a classroom teacher;

(ii) as a result of a subsequent determination by the relevant body, he is placed on a higher point on the pay scale set out either in paragraph 17.3 or in paragraph 19.2, or he first becomes entitled to be paid on the pay scale set out in paragraph 19.2, and the value of that point combined with any TLR or SEN allowance awarded to him equals or exceeds his original salary; or

(iii) as a result of a subsequent determination by the relevant body, he is awarded a TLR or a SEN allowance or both, and the combined value of that payment or allowance or payment and allowance and his new pay point equals or exceeds his original salary;

(c) in the case of a teacher affected by a determination within sub-paragraphs 1(d) to 1(h), the value of his point on the leadership pay spine, the advanced skills teachers' pay spine or the excellent teachers' salary range equals or exceeds his original salary; or

(d) the teacher's employment at the school ends other than in circumstances to which paragraph 45 or 46 applies,

whichever is the first to occur.

47.7 Payment of the safeguarded sum must be discontinued whilst the teacher occupies a post as a member of the leadership group, as an advanced skills teacher or as an excellent teacher in the temporary absence of the post-holder but reinstated thereafter, unless, in the meantime, any of the events specified in sub-paragraph 6 occurs.

47.8 In this paragraph "original salary" means-

(a) in the case of a member of the leadership group, the value of the point on the leadership pay spine to which the teacher was entitled immediately before the implementation of the determination;

(b) in the case of an advanced skills teacher, the value of the point on the pay spine for advanced skills teachers in paragraph 29.1 to which the teacher was entitled immediately before the implementation of the determination; and

(c) in the case of an excellent teacher, the salary to which the teacher was entitled immediately before the implementation of the determination,

taking into account any annual determination made under paragraph 4.1 but not yet implemented.

Reduction of ISR prior to 1st September 2005

SECTION 2

48.1 This paragraph applies to a head teacher whose salary was safeguarded under paragraph 7.3(e)(ii) of the 2004 Document.

48.2.1 The relevant body must re-determine the value of the safeguarded sum at the time of each annual determination of remuneration made under paragraph 4.1, taking into account both the value of the old point at the date of that determination and the value of the point on the leadership pay spine at which the head teacher is then placed.

48.2.2 Any change to the value of the safeguarded sum must be included in the notification given under paragraph 4.4.

48.3 Subject to paragraph 5.1, the head teacher must be paid the safeguarded sum until-

(a) he ceases to be a head teacher;

(b) as a result of a determination by the relevant body, he is placed on a higher point on the leadership pay spine than the original point; or

(c) the head teacher's employment at the school ends other than in circumstances to which paragraph 45 or 46 applies,

whichever is the first to occur.

Part-time teachers

Interpretation

49.1.1 In this paragraph-

"pro rata principle" means that proportion of total remuneration which corresponds to the number of hours that the teacher is employed in that capacity during the course of the school's timetabled teaching week as a proportion of the total number of hours in the school's timetabled teaching week; (and for this purpose "total remuneration" means the remuneration that would be payable to that person if he were employed in the same post on a full-time basis; and "the school's timetabled teaching week" means the aggregate period of time in the school timetable during which pupils are normally taught).

49.1.2 When a relevant body is required to determine the salary of a part-time teacher in accordance with the pro rata principle it must do so not only in relation to those hours that a part-time teacher normally works under his contract of employment but also in relation to any additional hours such a teacher may agree to work from time to time at the request of the head teacher or in the case where the part-time teacher is a head teacher, the relevant body.

Determination of remuneration of new part-time teachers

49.2 The salary and allowances, if any, of any person appointed as a part-time teacher on or after 1st September 2008 must be determined in accordance with the pro rata principle.

Re-determination of salary of existing part-time teachers

49.3.1 The salary of any person employed as a part-time teacher on 31st August 2008 must be re-determined by the relevant body in accordance with this sub-paragraph with effect from 1st September 2008.

49.3.2 The relevant body must-

(a) determine the salary that the teacher would have been entitled to receive with effect from 1st September 2008, had there been no change to the arrangements for determining the remuneration of part-time teachers, excluding any award of additional points on the applicable scale or spine payable with effect from 1st September 2008 ("original salary");

(b) re-calculate the original salary in accordance with the pro rata principle ("new salary");

(c) where the new salary is less than the original salary, calculate the safeguarded sum (the difference between the two);

(d) where the teacher is awarded one or more additional points with effect from the 1st September 2008, add the value of those points to the new salary ("revised new salary").

Safeguarding of salary of existing part-time teachers

49.4.1 Where, following the re-determination under sub-paragraph 3, the teacher's new salary is less than his original salary and he is not awarded any additional points with effect from 1st September 2008, he must be paid the safeguarded sum in addition to his new salary.

49.4.2 Where, following the re-determination under sub-paragraph 3, the teacher's new salary is less than his original salary and he is awarded one or more additional points with effect from 1st September 2008,

(a) if his revised new salary is less than the combined total of his original salary and the safeguarded sum, the teacher must be paid the safeguarded sum in addition to his revised new salary;

(b) if his revised new salary exceeds the combined total of his original salary and the safeguarded sum, the teacher must not be paid the safeguarded sum.

49.4.3 Within one month of any determination which results in the teacher being entitled to be paid a safeguarded sum under sub-paragraph 4.1 or 4.2(a), the relevant body must notify the part-time teacher in writing of that fact and of-

(a) the reason for the determination;

(b) the teacher's original salary;

(c) the safeguarded sum;

(d) (i) the date on which the safeguarded sum will cease to be payable (31st August 2011); or

(ii) in the case of a teacher employed as a part-time teacher for a fixed period or under a fixed-term contract, the date or the circumstance the occurrence of which will bring that fixed period or fixed-term contract to an end.

49.4.4 Subject to paragraph 5.1, the safeguarded sum must be paid to the part-time teacher until-

(a) 31st August 2011;

(b) in the case where a teacher is employed as a part-time teacher for a fixed period or under a fixed-term contract, the date on which that fixed period or fixed-term contract expires;

(c) his salary is increased following a subsequent determination and the increase in salary equals or exceeds the safeguarded sum;

(d) he ceases to be a part-time teacher; or

(e) his employment at the school ends, other than in circumstances to which paragraph 45 or 46 applies,

whichever is the first to occur.

Review of allowances of existing part-time teachers

49.5.1 Any allowances paid to a person employed as a part-time teacher on 31st August 2008 must be reviewed by the relevant body in accordance with this sub-paragraph.

49.5.2 The relevant body must-

(a) determine the allowance that the teacher would have been entitled to receive with effect from 1st September 2008, had there been no change to the arrangements for determining the remuneration of part-time teachers ("original allowance"); and

(b) re-calculate the original allowance in accordance with the pro rata principle.

49.5.3 Where the re-calculation of the original allowance under sub-paragraph 5.2(b) produces a figure which exceeds the original allowance, the relevant body must increase the allowance paid to the teacher by the amount of the difference between the two, with effect from 1st September 2008.

49.5.4 Where the re-calculation of the original allowance under sub-paragraph 5.2(b) produces a figure which is less than the original allowance, the relevant body must continue to pay the teacher the original allowance, with effect from 1st September 2008 until-

(a) 31st August 2011;

(b) in the case where a teacher is employed as a part-time teacher for a fixed period or under a fixed-term contract, the date on which that fixed period or fixed-term contract expires;

(c) his salary is increased following a subsequent determination and the increase in salary equals or exceeds the safeguarded sum;

(d) he ceases to be a part-time teacher; or

(e) his employment at the school ends, other than in circumstances to which paragraph 45 or 46 applies,

whichever is the first to occur.

SECTION 2

Review of safeguarded sums paid to existing part-time teachers under paragraph 46

49.6.1 Any safeguarded sum paid to a person employed as a part-time teacher on 31st August 2008 under paragraph 46("original safeguarded sum") must be reviewed by the relevant body in accordance with this sub-paragraph.

49.6.2 The relevant body must re-calculate the existing safeguarded sum in accordance with the pro rata principle.

49.6.3 Where the re-calculation of the existing safeguarded sum under sub-paragraph 6.2 produces a figure which exceeds the existing safeguarded sum, the relevant body must increase the safeguarded sum paid to the teacher by the amount of the difference between the two, with effect from 1st September 2008.

49.6.4 Where the re-calculation of the existing safeguarded sum under sub-paragraph 6.2 produces a figure which is less than the existing safeguarded sum, the relevant body must continue to pay the teacher the existing safeguarded sum, with effect from 1st September 2008 until whichever of the events listed in paragraph 46.4 occurs first.

Teachers employed on a short notice basis

50.1 Teachers employed on a day-to-day or other short notice basis must be paid in accordance with the provisions of this Document on a daily basis calculated on the assumption that a full working year consists of 195 days, periods of employment for less than a day being calculated pro rata.

50.2 A teacher to whom sub-paragraph 1 applies and who is employed by the same authority throughout a period of 12 months beginning in August or September must not be paid more by way of remuneration in respect of that period than he would have received had he been in regular employment throughout the period.

Residential duties

51. Any payment to teachers for residential duties must be determined by the relevant body.

Additional payments

52. The relevant body may make such payments as they see fit to a teacher, including a head teacher, in respect of-

(a) continuing professional development undertaken outside the school day;

(b) activities relating to the provision of initial teacher training as part of the ordinary conduct of the school;

(c) participation in out-of-school hours learning activity agreed between the teacher and the head teacher or, in the case of the head teacher, between the head teacher and the relevant body.

Recruitment and retention incentives and benefits

53.1 Subject to sub-paragraphs 2 and 3, the relevant body and, where it is the teacher's employer, the authority, may make such payments or provide other financial assistance, support or benefits to a teacher as it considers to be necessary as an incentive for the recruitment of new teachers and the retention in their service of existing teachers.

53.2 An incentive for the recruitment of a new teacher that consists of periodic payments or the provision of other benefits over a period of time may only be awarded for a fixed period not exceeding three years and must not be renewed.

53.3 An incentive for the retention of an existing teacher that consists of periodic payments or the provision of other benefits over a period of time may only be awarded for a fixed period not exceeding three years and may, in exceptional circumstances, be renewed.

53.4 In this paragraph "allowance" means a recruitment and retention allowance, or other assistance, support or benefit awarded by the relevant body as an incentive for the recruitment of new teachers or the retention in its service of existing teachers.

General Teaching Councils' fee allowance

54.1 The relevant body must pay the sum of £33 per year to a teacher who is required to be registered with the General Teaching Council for England or the General Teaching Council for Wales, in respect of the annual registration fee, where such a fee is payable by that teacher.

54.2 Before making a determination under sub-paragraph 1 the relevant body must take reasonable steps to satisfy itself that the teacher has not received a payment in respect of that year under that provision from any other relevant body.

54.3 A local education authority must upon request take reasonable steps to provide a relevant body with information as to whether or not a teacher who is or has been employed at a school or as an unattached teacher within that authority has received a payment under sub-paragraph 1.

54.4 Paragraph 49 of this Document does not apply to this allowance.

Salary sacrifice arrangements

55.1 For the purposes of this paragraph, the term "salary sacrifice arrangement" means any arrangement under which the teacher gives up the right to receive part of his gross salary in return for the employer's agreement to provide him with a benefit-in-kind under any of the following schemes-

(a) a child care voucher or other child care benefit scheme;

(b) a cycle or cyclist's safety equipment scheme; or

(c) a mobile telephone scheme; and

that benefit-in-kind is exempt from income tax (73).

55.2 Where the employer operates a salary sacrifice arrangement, the teacher may participate in any such arrangement and his gross salary may be reduced accordingly for the duration of his participation in it.

55.3 Participation in any salary sacrifice arrangement has no effect upon the determination of any safeguarded sum to which the teacher may be entitled under any provision of this Document.

(73) The Income Tax (Earning and Pensions) Act 2003 (2003 c.1) provides that no liability to income tax arises in respect of the provision for an employee of any of these benefits-in-kind, where the specified conditions are met.

Conditions of Employment
PART 8 – General

SECTION 2

Conditions to be included

56.1 The conditions of employment of all head teachers include the conditions set out in Part 9, the conditions of employment of deputy head teachers and assistant head teachers include the conditions set out in Part 10 and the conditions of employment of advanced skills teachers and excellent teachers include the conditions set out in Part 11.

56.2 Subject to paragraphs 41.6, 44.2, 44.3 and sub-paragraph 3, the conditions of employment of all teachers other than head teachers include the conditions set out in Part 12.

56.3 The conditions set out in paragraph 77 do not apply to deputy head teachers, assistant head teachers or advanced skills teachers but such a teacher must in addition to the hours during which he is required to perform his duties as specified by the head teacher work such reasonable hours as may be needed to enable him effectively to discharge his professional duties.

56.4 Nothing in this Document is to be taken to conflict with Council Directive 93/104/EC of 23rd November 1993 concerning certain aspects of the organisation of working time(74).

(74) O.J. No.L307, 13.12.93 p.18 which was implemented by the Working Time Regulations 1998 (S.I. 1998/1833).

PART 9 – Conditions of Employment of Head Teachers

Overriding requirements

57.1 A head teacher must carry out his professional duties in accordance with and subject to-

(a) the provisions of the Education Acts;

(b) any orders and regulations having effect under the Education Acts;

(c) the instrument of government of the school of which he is head teacher;

(d) where the school is a voluntary, foundation or foundation special school, any trust deed that applies to the school;

(e) any scheme prepared by the authority under section 48 of the School Standards and Framework Act 1998([75]).

57.2 A head teacher must carry out his duties in accordance with and subject to the following (to the extent to which they are not inconsistent with paragraphs 58 to 63)-

(a) in the case of a school which has a delegated budget-

(i) any rules, regulations or policies laid down by the governing body for which they are responsible under their powers as derived from the Education Acts; and

(ii) any rules, regulations or policies laid down by the authority with respect to matters for which the governing body is not so responsible;

(b) in any other case, any rules, regulations or policies laid down by his employers; and

(c) the terms of his appointment.

57.3 In carrying out his professional duties, including in particular his duties under paragraph 60.3.1, a head teacher must have regard to the desirability of teachers at the school being able to achieve a satisfactory balance between the time required to discharge their

(75) 1998 c.31 as amended by section 40 and Schedule 3 to the Act.

SECTION 2

professional duties including in particular, in the case of teachers to whom paragraph 77 applies, their duties under paragraph 77.13 and the time required to pursue their personal interests outside work.

General functions

58. Subject to paragraph 57.1, a head teacher is responsible for the leadership, internal organisation, management and control of the school.

Consultation

59. In carrying out his duties a head teacher must consult, where this is appropriate, with the authority, the governing body, the staff of the school and the parents of its pupils.

Professional duties

60.1 The professional duties of a head teacher include-

School aims

60.2 formulating the overall aims and objectives of the school and policies for their implementation;

Appointment of staff

60.3 participating in the selection and appointment of the teaching and support staff of the school;

Management of staff

60.4.1 deploying and managing all teaching and support staff of the school and allocating particular duties to them (including such duties of the head teacher as may properly be delegated to a deputy head teacher, assistant head teacher or other member of the staff) in a manner consistent with their conditions of employment, having regard to the nature and extent of their management responsibilities, and maintaining a reasonable balance for each teacher between work carried out in school and work carried out elsewhere;

60.4.2 considering in particular in relation to such allocation of duties how far the duties of the head teacher may be delegated to any deputy head teacher or assistant head teacher;

60.4.3 ensuring, save in exceptional circumstances that a teacher is assigned in the school timetable to every class or group of pupils-

(a) in the first, second, third and fourth key stages, for foundation and other core subjects and religious education; and

(b) in the preliminary stage;

60.4.4 ensuring that the duty of providing cover for absent teachers is shared equitably among all teachers in the school (including the head teacher), taking account of their teaching and other duties and of the desirability of not using a teacher at the school until all other reasonable means of providing cover have been exhausted;

60.4.5 ensuring that teachers at the school receive information they need in order to carry out their professional duties effectively;

60.4.6 enabling advanced skills teachers to fulfil their outreach duties under paragraph 68.2 by taking reasonable steps to arrange or permit such work–

(a) in the case of such teachers at the school, at the school or elsewhere; and

(b) in the case of such teachers from other schools working with teachers from the school, at the school or elsewhere;

60.4.7 reporting to the chair of governors annually on the professional development of all teachers at the school;

60.4.8 advising the governing body on the adoption of effective procedures to deal with incompetent teachers;

60.4.9 keeping the governing body informed of the general operation of such procedures; and

60.4.10 advising the governing body on the formulation and adoption of their pay policy in accordance with paragraph 3;

Liaison with staff unions and associations

60.5 maintaining relationships with organisations representing teachers and other persons on the staff of the school;

Curriculum

60.6.1 determining, organising and implementing an appropriate curriculum for the school, having regard to the needs, experience, interests, aptitudes and stage of development of the pupils and the resources available to the school; and his duty under section 69 of the School Standards and Framework Act 1998([76]) and section 79(3) of the Act;

60.6.2 securing that all pupils in attendance at the school take part in daily collective worship in accordance with section 70 of the School Standards and Framework Act 1998;

Review

60.7 keeping under review the work and organisation of the school;

Standards of teaching and learning

60.8 evaluating the standards of teaching and learning in the school, and ensuring that proper standards of professional performance are established and maintained;

Appraisal or review of performance, training, development and induction of staff

60.9.1 supervising and participating in arrangements made in accordance with the 2002 Regulations or the 2006 Regulations for the appraisal or review of the performance of teachers in the school; participating in arrangements made for the appraisal or review of his performance as head teacher, and that of other head teachers who are the responsibility of the same appraising or reviewing body in accordance with such regulations; participating in the identification of areas in which he would benefit from further training and undergoing such training;

60.9.2 ensuring that all staff in the school have access to advice, training and developmental opportunities appropriate to their needs, including needs identified in statements of objectives or in appraisal statements, where teachers are subject to the 2002 Regulations, or in planning and review statements, where teachers are subject to the 2006 Regulations, in accordance with the policies of the maintaining authority and governing body;

60.9.3 ensuring that newly-qualified teachers and those returning to teaching after a break in service have access to adequate support in their first year of service or resumed service;

(76) 1998 c.31. Section 69 was amended by section 215 of and Schedule 21 to the Act.

60.9.4 being responsible for the supervision and training of teachers during their induction periods in accordance with the Induction Regulations, and making a recommendation at the end of such induction periods as to whether such teachers have met the prescribed induction standards as required by those Regulations;

60.9.5 ensuring that teachers serving induction periods under the Induction Regulations do not teach for more than 90% of the time that a teacher at that school who does not receive payments in respect of additional duties or responsibilities would be expected to teach;

Threshold assessment

60.10.1 satisfying himself whether a teacher at the school who applies for a post-threshold teacher assessment under paragraph 21 meets the core standards and, where he is so satisfied, assessing whether that teacher has met the post-threshold teacher standards throughout the relevant period;

60.10.2 where he is not satisfied that the teacher meets the core standards or, having gone on to assess the teacher against the post-threshold teacher standards, he determines that the teacher has not met the post-threshold teacher standards throughout the relevant period, explaining to the teacher the reasons for his decision and giving him advice about those aspects of his performance which must be improved in order to meet those standards;

60.10.3 the professional duties of a head teacher under this sub-paragraph must not be delegated to a deputy or assistant head teacher, although pursuant to paragraph 65.4 they may be exercised by a deputy head teacher in the head teacher's absence from the school;

Advanced skills teacher and excellent teacher assessment

60.11.1 satisfying himself, in connection with an application by a teacher at the school for assessment against the relevant standards set out in Annex 1, that the teacher meets the standards which apply to any person on the same pay scale or pay spine as the applicant or, where the applicant is an excellent teacher, any person on an excellent teacher's salary and, where he is not so satisfied, explaining to the teacher the reasons for his decision and giving him advice about the aspects of his performance which must be improved in order to meet those standards;

60.11.2 providing, in connection with an application for an assessment by an assessor against the relevant standards set out in Annex 1 by a teacher at the school or a teacher who was previously employed at the school-

(a) such documents, other information and assistance as may reasonably be requested by the teacher; and

(b) such assistance as may reasonably be requested by the assessor;

60.11.3 the professional duties of a head teacher under this sub-paragraph must not be delegated to a deputy or assistant head teacher, although, pursuant to paragraph 65.4, they may be exercised by a deputy head teacher in the head teacher's absence from the school.

Management information

60.12 providing information about the work and performance of the staff employed at the school where this is relevant to their future employment;

Pupil progress

60.13 ensuring that the progress of the pupils of the school is monitored and recorded;

Pastoral care

60.14 determining and ensuring the implementation of a policy for the pastoral care of the pupils;

Discipline

60.15.1 determining, in accordance with any written statement of general principles provided for him by the governing body, measures to be taken with a view to promoting, among the pupils, self-discipline and proper regard for authority, encouraging good behaviour on the part of the pupils, securing that the standard of behaviour of the pupils is acceptable and otherwise regulating the conduct of the pupils; making such measures generally known within the school, and ensuring that they are implemented; and

60.15.2 ensuring the maintenance of good order and discipline at all times during the school day (including the midday break) when pupils are present on the school premises and whenever the pupils are engaged in authorised school activities, whether on the school premises or elsewhere;

Relations with parents

60.16 making arrangements for parents to be given regular information about the school curriculum, the progress of their children and other matters affecting the school, so as to promote common understanding of its aims;

Relations with other bodies

60.17 promoting effective relationships with persons and bodies outside the school;

Relations with the governing body

60.18 advising and assisting the governing body of the school in the exercise of their functions, including (without prejudice to any rights he may have as a governor of the school) attending meetings of the governing body and making such reports to them in connection with the discharge of his functions as they may properly require either on a regular basis or from time to time;

Relations with the authority

60.19 providing for liaison and co-operation with the officers of the maintaining authority; making such reports to the authority in connection with the discharge of his functions as they may properly require, either on a regular basis or from time to time;

Relations with other educational establishments

60.20 liaising with other schools and further education establishments with which the school has a relationship;

Resources

60.21 allocating, controlling and accounting for those financial and material resources of the school which are under the control of the head teacher;

Premises

60.22 making arrangements, if so required by the authority or the governing body (as appropriate), for the security and effective supervision of the school buildings and their contents and of the school grounds; and ensuring (if so required) that any lack of maintenance is promptly reported to the authority or, if appropriate, the governing body;

Absence

60.23 arranging for a deputy head teacher or other suitable person to assume responsibility for the discharge of his functions as head teacher at any time when he is absent from the school;

Teaching

60.24 participating, to such extent as may be appropriate having regard to his leadership and other functions and duties, in the teaching of pupils at the school, including the provision of cover for absent teachers but to no greater extent than if he were a teacher to whom paragraph 75.9.2 applies.

Dedicated headship time

61. A head teacher is entitled to a reasonable amount of time during school sessions, having regard to his teaching responsibilities, for the purpose of discharging his leadership and management responsibilities.

Guaranteed planning and preparation time

62. A head teacher who participates in the teaching of pupils at the school has the same entitlement to planning and preparation time as a deputy or assistant head teacher has under paragraph 66 (treating the reference in that paragraph to "timetabled teaching time" as a reference to the aggregate period of time in the school timetable during which the head teacher has assigned himself to teach pupils).

Daily break

63. A head teacher is entitled to a break of reasonable length in the course of each school day, and must arrange for a suitable person to assume responsibility for the discharge of his functions as head teacher during that break.

Working days

64. No head teacher may be required to work any Saturday, Sunday or public holiday unless his contract of employment expressly provides for this.

PART 10 – Conditions of Employment of Deputy Head Teachers and Assistant Head Teachers

SECTION 2

Professional duties

65.1 A person appointed as a deputy or assistant head teacher in a school, in addition to carrying out the professional duties of a teacher other than a head teacher (as described in Part 12) including those duties particularly assigned to him by the head teacher, must-

65.2 play a major role under the overall direction of the head teacher in-

(a) formulating the aims and objectives of the school;

(b) establishing the policies through which they are to be achieved;

(c) managing staff and resources to that end; and

(d) monitoring progress towards their achievement;

65.3 undertake any professional duties of the head teacher reasonably delegated to him by the head teacher;

65.4 in the case of a deputy head teacher only, undertake to the extent required by the head teacher or the relevant body or, in the case of a foundation, voluntary aided or foundation special school, the governing body, the professional duties of the head teacher in the event of his absence from the school; and

65.5 be entitled to a break of reasonable length as near to the middle of each school day as is reasonably practicable.

Guaranteed planning and preparation time

66.1 A deputy head teacher or an assistant head teacher is entitled to reasonable periods of time ("PPA time") to enable him to discharge his duties under paragraphs 75.1.1, 75.1.3 and 75.3.

66.2 PPA time must amount to not less than 10% of the deputy or assistant head teacher's timetabled teaching time (and for this purpose "timetabled teaching time", in relation to a deputy or assistant head teacher, means the aggregate period of time in the school timetable during which the deputy or assistant head teacher has been assigned by the head teacher in the school timetable to teach pupils).

66.3 PPA time must be provided in units of not less than half an hour during those parts of the school timetable in which pupils are taught the core and other foundation subjects or religious education.

66.4 No deputy or assistant head teacher may be required to carry out any other duties, including the provision of cover in accordance with paragraph 75.9, during his PPA time.

Working days

67. No deputy or assistant head teacher may be required to work on any Saturday, Sunday or public holiday unless his contract of employment expressly provides for this.

PART 11 – Conditions of Employment of Advanced Skills Teachers and Excellent Teachers

Professional duties of advanced skills teachers

68.1 A teacher who is appointed as an advanced skills teacher, in addition to carrying out the professional duties of a teacher other than a head teacher (as described in Part 12) including those duties particularly assigned to him by the head teacher, may be required to carry out the following professional duties-

(a) participating in initial teacher training;

(b) participating in the induction and mentoring of newly qualified teachers;

(c) advising other teachers on classroom organisation and teaching methods;

(d) producing high quality teaching materials;

(e) disseminating to other teachers materials relating to best practice and educational research;

(f) advising on the provision of continuous professional development;

(g) participating in the appraisal or review of performance of other teachers;

(h) helping teachers who are experiencing difficulties;

(i) producing high quality resources and materials, including video recordings of lessons, for dissemination in their own school and other schools.

68.2 An advanced skills teacher must normally spend 20% of his time undertaking outreach work carrying out the duties in sub paragraph 1 with or for the benefit of teachers or trainee teachers from other schools, whether at the school of the advanced skills teacher, at that of the other teachers, in higher education institutions, at facilities of the authority or elsewhere.

SECTION 2

Professional duties of excellent teachers

69. A teacher who is appointed to an excellent teacher post, in addition to carrying out the professional duties of a teacher other than a head teacher (as described in Part 12), including those duties particularly assigned to him by the head teacher, may be required to carry out the following professional duties-

(a) participating in the induction of newly qualified teachers;

(b) participating in the professional mentoring of other teachers;

(c) sharing good practice through demonstration lessons;

(d) helping other teachers to develop their expertise in planning, preparation and assessment;

(e) helping other teachers to evaluate the impact of their teaching practice on pupils;

(f) undertaking classroom observations to assist and support the performance management process; and

(g) helping other teachers, including those on capability procedures, improve their teaching practice.

Daily break

70. An advanced skills teacher and an excellent teacher are entitled to a break of reasonable length as near to the middle of each school day as is reasonably practicable.

Guaranteed planning and preparation time

71. An advanced skills teacher and an excellent teacher have the same entitlement to planning and preparation time as a deputy or assistant head teacher has under paragraph 66.

Working days

72. No advanced skills teacher or excellent teacher may be required to work on any Saturday, Sunday or public holiday unless his contract of employment expressly provides for this.

PART 12 – Conditions of Employment of Teachers other than Head Teachers

Exercise of general professional duties

73.1 Subject to paragraphs 41.6 and 44.2, a teacher who is not a head teacher must carry out the professional duties of a teacher as circumstances may require-

73.1.1 if he is employed as a teacher in a school, under the reasonable direction of the head teacher of that school;

73.1.2 if he is employed by an authority on terms under which he is not assigned to any one school, under the reasonable direction of that authority and of the head teacher of any school in which he may for the time being be required to work as a teacher.

73.2 A teacher who has failed satisfactorily to complete an induction period and who is employed pursuant to regulation 18(5) of the Induction Regulations in relation to England or regulation 16(5) of the Induction Regulations in relation to Wales must only carry out such limited teaching duties as the Secretary of State determines pursuant to that regulation.

Exercise of particular duties

74.1 Subject to paragraphs 41.6, 44.2, 44.3 and 74.2 a teacher employed as a teacher (other than a head teacher) in a school must perform, in accordance with any directions which may reasonably be given to him by the head teacher from time to time, such particular duties as may reasonably be assigned to him.

74.2 A teacher employed by an authority on terms such as those described in paragraph 73.1.2 must perform, in accordance with any direction which may reasonably be given to him from time to time by the authority or by the head teacher of any school in which he may for the time being be required to work as a teacher, such particular duties as may reasonably be assigned to him.

Professional duties

75. Subject to paragraphs 41.6, 44.2 and 44.3, the following duties are deemed to be included in the professional duties which a teacher (other than a head teacher) may be required to perform-

SECTION 2

Teaching

75.1 In each case having regard to the curriculum for the school, and with a view to promoting the development of the abilities and aptitudes of the pupils in any class or group assigned to him-

75.1.1 planning and preparing courses and lessons;

75.1.2 teaching, according to their educational needs, the pupils assigned to him, including the setting and marking of work to be carried out by the pupil in school and elsewhere;

75.1.3 assessing, recording and reporting on the development, progress and attainment of pupils;

Other activities

75.2.1 promoting the general progress and well-being of individual pupils and of any class or group of pupils assigned to him;

75.2.2 providing guidance and advice to pupils on educational and social matters and on their further education and future careers, including information about sources of more expert advice on specific questions; making relevant records and reports;

75.2.3 making records of and reports on the personal and social needs of pupils;

75.2.4 communicating and consulting with the parents of pupils;

75.2.5 communicating and co-operating with persons or bodies outside the school; and

75.2.6 participating in meetings arranged for any of the purposes described above;

Assessments and reports

75.3 providing or contributing to oral and written assessments, reports and references relating to individual pupils and groups of pupils;

Appraisal or review of performance

75.4 participating in arrangements made in accordance with the 2002 Regulations or the 2006 Regulations for the appraisal or review of his performance and that of other teachers;

Review, induction, further training and development

75.5.1 reviewing from time to time his methods of teaching and programmes of work;

75.5.2 participating in arrangements for his further training and professional development as a teacher including undertaking training and professional development which aim to meet needs identified in statements of objectives or in appraisal statements where teachers are subject to the 2002 Regulations, or in planning and review statements where teachers are subject to the 2006 Regulations;

75.5.3 in the case of a teacher serving an induction period pursuant to the Induction Regulations, participating in arrangements for his supervision and training;

Educational methods

75.6 advising and co-operating with the head teacher and other teachers (or any one or more of them) on the preparation and development of courses of study, teaching materials, teaching programmes, methods of teaching and assessment and pastoral arrangements;

Discipline, health and safety

75.7 maintaining good order and discipline among the pupils and safeguarding their health and safety both when they are authorised to be on the school premises and when they are engaged in authorised school activities elsewhere;

Staff meetings

75.8 participating in meetings at the school which relate to the curriculum for the school or the administration or organisation of the school, including pastoral arrangements;

Cover

75.9.1 subject to sub-paragraph 9.2, supervising and so far as practicable teaching any pupils whose teacher is not available to teach them;

75.9.2 except in the case of a teacher employed wholly or mainly for the purpose of providing such cover, no teacher may be required to provide such cover for more than 38 hours in any school year;

External examinations

75.10.1 participating in arrangements for preparing pupils for external examinations, assessing pupils for the purposes of such examinations and recording and reporting such assessments; and

SECTION 2

participating in arrangements for pupils presentation for, and conducting, such examinations;

75.10.2 sub-paragraph 10.1 does not require a teacher routinely to participate in any arrangements that do not call for the exercise of a teacher's professional skills and judgement, such as invigilation;

Management

75.11.1 contributing to the selection for appointment and professional development of other teachers and support staff, including the induction and assessment of new teachers and teachers serving induction periods pursuant to the Induction Regulations;

75.11.2 assisting the head teacher in carrying out threshold assessments of other teachers for whom he has management responsibility;

75.11.3 co-ordinating or managing the work of other staff; and

75.11.4 taking such part as may be required of him in the review, development and management of activities relating to the curriculum, organisation and pastoral functions of the school;

Administration

75.12.1 participating in administrative and organisational tasks related to such duties as are described above, including the direction or supervision of persons providing support for the teachers in the school; and

75.12.2 attending assemblies, registering the attendance of pupils and supervising pupils, whether these duties are to be performed before, during or after school sessions.

75.12.3 Sub-paragraph 12.1 does not require a teacher routinely to undertake tasks of a clerical or administrative nature which do not call for the exercise of a teacher's professional skills and judgment.

75.12.4 Without prejudice to the generality of sub-paragraph 12.3, Annex 3 contains a list of tasks falling within the scope of that paragraph.

Management time

76. A teacher with leadership or management responsibilities is entitled, so far as is reasonably practicable, to a reasonable amount of time during school sessions for the purpose of discharging those responsibilities.

Working time

77.1 The provisions of this paragraph do not apply to-

(a) deputy head teachers, assistant head teachers, advanced skills teachers or teachers in receipt of an acting allowance for carrying out the duties of a head teacher, deputy head teacher or assistant head teacher pursuant to paragraph 41;

(b) unattached teachers in charge of pupil referral units whose remuneration is determined in accordance with the provisions applicable to head teachers pursuant to paragraph 44;

(c) unattached teachers (other than those in charge of pupil referral units) whose remuneration is determined in accordance with the provisions applicable to a member of the leadership group pursuant to paragraph 44.

77.2 No teacher may be required to work on any Saturday, Sunday or public holiday unless his contract of employment expressly provides for this.

77.3 A teacher employed full-time must be available for work for 195 days in any school year, of which-

(a) 190 days must be days on which he may be required to teach pupils and perform other duties; and

(b) 5 days must be days on which he may only be required to perform other duties; and

those 195 days must be specified by his employer or, if his employer so directs, by the head teacher.

77.4 A teacher employed full-time must be available to perform such duties at such times and such places as may be specified by the head teacher (or, where the teacher is not assigned to any one school, by his employer or the head teacher of any school in which he may for the time being be required to work as a teacher) for 1265 hours in any school year, those hours to be allocated reasonably throughout those days in the school year on which he is required to be available for work.

77.5 Sub-paragraph 3 of this paragraph does not apply to a teacher employed full-time wholly or mainly to teach or perform other duties in relation to pupils in a residential establishment.

77.6 Sub-paragraph 4 applies to a teacher employed part-time, except that the number of hours he must be available for work in any school year must be that proportion of 1265 hours which corresponds to the proportion of total remuneration he is entitled to be paid pursuant to paragraph 49.

77.7 Subject to sub-paragraph 8, no teacher employed part-time may be required to be available for work on any day of the week or part of any day of the week that he is not normally required to be available for work under his contract of employment (whether it is for the purposes of teaching pupils and performing other duties or for the sole purpose of performing other duties).

77.8 Subject to sub-paragraphs 6 and 9, a teacher employed part-time may be required to carry out duties, other than teaching pupils, outside school sessions on any day that he is normally required to be available for work (whether he is normally required to be available for work for the whole of that day or for only part of that day).

77.9 The total amount of time that the teacher may be required to be available to carry out duties, other than teaching pupils, outside school sessions under sub-paragraph 8, when expressed as a proportion of the total amount of time that he would be required to be available for such work if he were employed in the same post on a full-time basis, must not exceed the equivalent of that proportion of total remuneration that he is entitled to be paid under paragraph 49.

77.10 No teacher may be required under his contract of employment as a teacher to undertake midday supervision.

77.11 A teacher who is required to be available for work for more than one school session on any school day must be allowed one break of reasonable length either between school sessions or between the hours of 12 noon and 2.00pm.

77.12 The amount of time a teacher spends taking the break referred to in sub-paragraph 11 or travelling to or from his place of work does not count towards the 1265 hours referred to in sub-paragraph 4 or the pro rata equivalent referred to in sub-paragraph 6, as the case may be.

77.13 In addition to the hours a teacher is required to be available for work under sub-paragraph 4 or sub-paragraph 6, as the case may be, a teacher must work such reasonable additional hours as may be necessary to enable him to discharge effectively his professional duties, including, in particular, his duties under paragraphs 75.1.1 and 75.1.3.

77.14 The employer must not determine how many of the additional hours referred to in sub-paragraph 13 must be worked or when these hours must be worked.

Guaranteed planning and preparation time

78.1 A teacher to whom paragraph 77 applies must be allowed, as part of the 1265 hours referred to in paragraph 77.4, or, in the case of a teacher employed part-time, as part of the pro rata equivalent referred to in paragraph 77.6, reasonable periods of time ("PPA time") to enable him to carry out his duties under paragraphs 75.1.1, 75.1.3 and 75.3.

78.2 PPA time must amount to not less than 10% of the teacher's timetabled teaching time (and for this purpose "timetabled teaching time", in relation to a teacher, means the aggregate period of time in the school timetable during which the teacher has been assigned by the head teacher in the school time-table to teach pupils).

78.3 PPA time must be provided in units of not less than half an hour during those parts of the school timetable in which pupils are taught the core and other foundation subjects or religious education.

78.4 Such a teacher must not be required to carry out any other duties, including the provision of cover in accordance with paragraph 75.9, during his PPA time.

Changes taking effect from 1st September 2009

79. The amendments made by Annex 4 to the provisions of this Section are to have effect from 1st September 2009.

SECTION 2

ANNEX 1 – Professional standards for post-threshold teachers, excellent teachers and advanced skills teachers

Interpretation

In the table below-

the letter "A" indicates an advanced skills teacher standard;

the letter "C" indicates a core standard;

the letter "E" indicates an excellent teacher standard;

the letter "P" indicates a post-threshold teacher standard;

"classroom" means any setting where teaching and learning take place;

"formative assessment" means the process by which a teacher and learner identify the learner's needs and teaching and learning activities are adapted in order to meet those needs;

"learners" is used instead of the term 'children and young people' when learning is the main focus of the standard and means all children and young people;

"lessons" or "sequences of lessons" means all teaching and learning activities, wherever they take place, whatever their nature and length, and however they might be organised;

"personalised learning" means learning which focuses on individual progress, for the purposes of enhancing achievement, participation and progress at school;

"subjects/curriculum areas" means all forms of organised learning across the curriculum;

"well-being", in relation to children and young people, means their-

(a) physical and mental health and emotional well-being;

(b) protection from harm and neglect;

(c) education, training and recreation;

(d) contribution to society; and

(e) social and economic well-being;

"workplace" means any educational establishment or other place where teaching and learning take place.

FRAMEWORK OF PROFESSIONAL STANDARDS FOR POST-THRESHOLD TEACHERS, EXCELLENT TEACHERS AND ADVANCED SKILLS TEACHERS

1. Professional attributes		
Post-threshold teachers (P)	**Excellent teachers (E)**	**Advanced skills teachers (A)**
Relationships with children and young people		
C1 Have high expectations of children and young people including a commitment to ensuring that they can achieve their full educational potential and to establishing fair, respectful, trusting, supportive and constructive relationships with them		
C2 Hold positive values and attitudes and adopt high standards of behaviour in their professional role		
Frameworks		
C3 Maintain an up-to-date knowledge and understanding of the professional duties of teachers and the statutory framework within which they work, and contribute to the development, implementation and evaluation of the policies and practice of their workplace, including those designed to promote equality of opportunity		
P1 Contribute significantly, where appropriate, to implementing workplace policies and practice and to promoting collective responsibility for their implementation		
	E1 Be willing to take a leading role in developing workplace policies and practice and in promoting collective responsibility for their implementation	**A1** Be willing to take on a strategic leadership role in developing workplace policies and practice and in promoting collective responsibility for their implementation in their own and other workplaces

1. Professional attributes		
Post-threshold teachers (P)	**Excellent teachers (E)**	**Advanced skills teachers (A)**
Communicating and working with others		
C4 Communicate effectively with children, young people and colleagues Communicate effectively with parents and carers, conveying timely and relevant information about attainment, objectives, progress and well-being Recognise that communication is a two-way process and encourage parents and carers to participate in discussions about the progress, development and well-being of children and young people		
C5 Recognise and respect the contributions that colleagues, parents and carers can make to the development and well-being of children and young people, and to raising their levels of attainment		
C6 Have a commitment to collaboration and co-operative working where appropriate		
Personal professional development		
C7 Evaluate their performance and be committed to improving their practice through appropriate professional development		
C8 Have a creative and constructively critical approach towards innovation; being prepared to adapt their practice where benefits and improvements are identified		
	E2 Research and evaluate innovative curricular practices and draw on research outcomes and other sources of external evidence to inform their own practice and that of colleagues	
C9 Act upon advice and feedback and be open to coaching and mentoring		

2. Professional knowledge and understanding		
Post-threshold teachers (P)	**Excellent teachers (E)**	**Advanced skills teachers (A)**
	Teaching and learning	
C10 Have a good, up to date working knowledge and understanding of a range of teaching, learning and behaviour management strategies and know how to use and adapt them, including how to personalise learning to provide opportunities for all learners to achieve their potential		
P2 Have an extensive knowledge and understanding of how to use and adapt a range of teaching, learning and behaviour management strategies, including how to personalise learning to provide opportunities for all learners to achieve their potential		
	E3 Have a critical understanding of the most effective teaching, learning and behaviour management strategies, and including how to select and use approaches that personalise learning to provide opportunities for all learners to achieve their potential	
	Assessment and monitoring	
C11 Know the assessment requirements and arrangements for the subjects/curriculum areas they teach, including those relating to public examinations and qualifications		
P3 Have an extensive knowledge and well-informed understanding of the assessment requirements and arrangements for the subjects/curriculum areas they teach, including those related to public examinations and qualifications		
P4 Have up-to-date knowledge and understanding of the different types of qualifications and specifications and their suitability for meeting learners' needs		
C12 Know a range of approaches to assessment, including the importance of formative assessment		
C13 Know how to use local and national statistical information to evaluate the effectiveness of their teaching, to monitor the progress of those they teach and to raise levels of attainment		
C14 Know how to use reports and other sources of external information related to assessment in order to provide learners with accurate and constructive feedback on their strengths, weaknesses, attainment, progress and areas for development, including action plans for improvement		

2. Professional knowledge and understanding		
Post-threshold teachers (P)	**Excellent teachers (E)**	**Advanced skills teachers (A)**
	E4 Know how to improve the effectiveness of assessment practice in the workplace, including how to analyse statistical information to evaluate the effectiveness of teaching and learning across the school	
Subjects and Curriculum		
C15 Have a secure knowledge and understanding of their subjects/curriculum areas and related pedagogy including: the contribution that their subjects/curriculum areas can make to cross-curricular learning; and recent relevant developments		
P5 Have a more developed knowledge and understanding of their subjects/curriculum areas and related pedagogy including how learning progresses within them		
	E5 Have an extensive and deep knowledge and understanding of their subjects/curriculum areas and related pedagogy gained for example through involvement in wider professional networks associated with their subjects/curriculum areas	
C16 Know and understand the relevant statutory and non-statutory curricula and frameworks, including those provided through the National Strategies, for their subjects/curriculum areas and other relevant initiatives across the age and ability range they teach		
Literacy, numeracy and ICT		
C17 Know how to use skills in literacy, numeracy and ICT to support their teaching and wider professional activities		
Achievement and diversity		
C18 Understand how children and young people develop and how the progress, rate of development and well-being of learners are affected by a range of developmental, social, religious, ethnic, cultural and linguistic influences		
C19 Know how to make effective personalised provision for those they teach, including those for whom English is an additional language or who have special educational needs or disabilities, and how to take practical account of diversity and promote equality and inclusion in their teaching		

2. Professional knowledge and understanding		
Post-threshold teachers (P)	**Excellent teachers (E)**	**Advanced skills teachers (A)**
	E6 Have an extensive knowledge on matters concerning equality, inclusion and diversity in teaching	
C20 Understand the roles of colleagues such as those having specific responsibilities for learners with special educational needs, disabilities and other individual learning needs, and the contributions they can make to the learning, development and well-being of children and young people		
C21 Know when to draw on the expertise of colleagues, such as those with responsibility for the safeguarding of children and young people and special educational needs and disabilities, and to refer to sources of information, advice and support from external agencies		
Health and well-being		
C22 Know the current legal requirements, national policies and guidance on the safeguarding and promotion of the well-being of children and young people		
C23 Know the local arrangements concerning the safeguarding of children and young people		
C24 Know how to identify potential child abuse or neglect and follow safeguarding procedures		
C25 Know how to identify and support children and young people whose progress, development or well-being is affected by changes or difficulties in their personal circumstances, and when to refer them to colleagues for specialist support		
P6 Have sufficient depth of knowledge and experience to be able to give advice on the development and well-being of children and young people		

3. Professional skills		
Post-threshold teachers (P)	**Excellent teachers (E)**	**Advanced skills teachers (A)**
	Planning	
C26 Plan for progression across the age and ability range they teach, designing effective learning sequences within lessons and across series of lessons informed by secure subject/curriculum knowledge		
P7 Be flexible, creative and adept at designing learning sequences within lessons and across lessons that are effective and consistently well-matched to learning objectives and the needs of learners and which integrate recent developments, including those relating to subject/curriculum knowledge		
	E7 Take a lead in planning collaboratively with colleagues in order to promote effective practice **Identify and explore links within and between subjects/curriculum areas in their planning**	
C27 Design opportunities for learners to develop their literacy, numeracy, ICT and thinking and learning skills appropriate within their phase and context		
C28 Plan, set and assess homework ,other out-of-class assignments and coursework for examinations, where appropriate, to sustain learners' progress and to extend and consolidate their learning		
	Teaching	
C29 Teach challenging, well-organised lessons and sequences of lessons across the age and ability range they teach in which they: use an appropriate range of teaching strategies and resources, including e-learning, which meet learners' needs and take practical account of diversity and promote equality and inclusion build on the prior knowledge and attainment of those they teach in order that learners meet learning objectives and make sustained progress develop concepts and processes which enable learners to apply new knowledge, understanding and skills, adapt their language to suit the learners they teach, introducing new ideas and concepts clearly, and using explanations, questions, discussions and plenaries effectively manage the learning of individuals, groups and whole classes effectively, modifying their teaching appropriately to suit the stage of the lesson and the needs of the learners		

3. Professional skills		
Post-threshold teachers (P)	**Excellent teachers (E)**	**Advanced skills teachers (A)**
C30 Teach engaging and motivating lessons informed by well-grounded expectations of learners and designed to raise levels of attainment		
P8 Have teaching skills which lead to learners achieving well relative to their prior attainment, making progress as good as, or better than, similar learners nationally		
	E8 Have teaching skills which lead to excellent results and outcomes	
	E9 Demonstrate excellent and innovative pedagogical practice	
Assessing, monitoring and giving feedback		
C31 Make effective use of an appropriate range of observation, assessment, monitoring and recording strategies as a basis for setting challenging learning objectives and monitoring learners' progress and levels of attainment		
	E10 Demonstrate excellent ability to assess and evaluate	
C32 Provide learners, colleagues, parents and carers with timely, accurate and constructive feedback on learners' attainment, progress and areas for development		
	E11 Have an excellent ability to provide learners, colleagues, parents and carers with timely, accurate and constructive feedback on learners' attainment, progress and areas for development that promotes pupil progress	
C33 Support and guide learners so that they can reflect on their learning, identify the progress they have made, set positive targets for improvement and become successful independent learners		
C34 Use assessment as part of their teaching to diagnose learners' needs, set realistic and challenging targets for improvement and plan future teaching		
Reviewing teaching and learning		
C35 Review the effectiveness of their teaching and its impact on learners' progress, attainment and well-being, refining their approaches where necessary		
C36 Review the impact of the feedback provided to learners and guide learners on how to improve their attainment		

3. Professional skills		
Post-threshold teachers (P)	**Excellent teachers (E)**	**Advanced skills teachers (A)**
	E12 Use local and national statistical data and other information, in order to provide (a) a comparative baseline for evaluating learners' progress and attainment, (b) a means of judging the effectiveness of their teaching, and (c) a basis for improving teaching and learning	
Learning environment		
C37 Establish a purposefu and safe learning environment which complies with current legal requirements, national policies and guidance on the safeguarding and well being of children and young people so that learners feel secure and sufficiently confident to make an active contribution to learning and to the school Make use of the local arrangements concerning the safeguarding of children and young people Identify and use opportunities to personalise and extend learning through out-of-school contexts where possible making links between in-school learning and learning in out-of-school contexts		
C38 Manage learners' behaviour constructively by establishing and maintaining a clear and positive framework for discipline, in line with the school's behaviour policy Use a range of behaviour management techniques and strategies, adapting them as necessary to promote the self-control and independence of learners		
C39 Promote learners' self-control, independence and co-operation through developing their social, emotional and behavioural skills		
Team Working and Collaboration		
C40 Work as a team member and identify opportunities for working with colleagues, managing their work where appropriate and sharing the development of effective practice with them		
P9 Promote collaboration and work effectively as a team member		

3. Professional skills		
Post-threshold teachers (P)	**Excellent teachers (E)**	**Advanced skills teachers (A)**
	E13 Work closely with leadership teams, taking a leading role in developing, implementing and evaluating policies and practice that contribute to school improvement	**A2** Be part of or work closely with leadership teams, taking a leadership role in developing, implementing and evaluating policies and practice in their own and other workplaces that contribute to school improvement
C41 Ensure that colleagues working with them are appropriately involved in supporting learning and understand the roles they are expected to fulfil		
P10 Contribute to the professional development of colleagues through coaching and mentoring, demonstrating effective practice, and providing advice and feedback		
	E14 Contribute to the professional development of colleagues using a broad range of techniques and skills appropriate to their needs so that they demonstrate enhanced and effective practice	
	E15 Make well-founded appraisals of situations upon which they are asked to advise, applying high level skills in classroom observation to evaluate and advise colleagues on their work and devising and implementing effective strategies to meet the learning needs of children and young people leading to improvements in pupil outcomes	
		A3 Possess the analytical, interpersonal and organisational skills necessary to work effectively with staff and leadership teams beyond their own school

ANNEX 2 – Standards for Chartered London teachers

The applicant must show how his knowledge, skills and expertise have a positive impact on teaching and learning for London education, through working individually and collegially to meet the following standards-

Pedagogy and pupil learning

1. Create and manage a classroom environment to ensure a secure and supportive achievement culture and behaviour strategy to meet the needs of London's diverse and mobile pupil population.

2. Apply a wide range of teaching and learning strategies to reduce individual barriers to learning and to meet the variety of pupil needs in London.

3. Develop and implement inclusive practices in a range of learning settings appropriate to the diversity of pupils in London and the complexity of their personal learning, including support for special educational needs, to raise pupils' achievements.

4. Progress partnerships within and beyond the classroom with support staff, teachers, other professionals, agencies and community resources, to promote pupils' achievements, learning, development and well-being.

5. Analyse and use relevant data to inform and promote the highest possible aspirations for pupils and to target expectations and actions to raise pupil achievements.

Subject, specialism and phase

6. Demonstrate ongoing development and application of subject, specialism and/or phase knowledge and expertise, drawing on opportunities and resources in London to enrich the learning experience.

7. Identify and use the knowledge and experiences that pupils, their families and other communities bring from outside the school to enrich curriculum development and teaching practices.

Whole school

8. Contribute to the development and application of whole school policies and activities, to extend opportunities for pupil and school achievements in London.

9. Promote and apply shared professional learning and other forms of support and development for teachers to learn and work together, taking account of teacher mobility, to strengthen collective knowledge and expertise across teachers in London.

Diversity, communities and cultures

10. Build on, extend and apply knowledge of the range of communities, cultures and sub-cultures in London, to inform and promote individual pupils' learning.

11. Promote and implement policies and practices that encourage mutual tolerance and respect for diversity, challenge discrimination and widen pupils' understanding of their contribution to society.

12. Demonstrate a capacity to deal constructively and sensitively with conflicting community and cultural values in classrooms and schools.

ANNEX 3 – Administrative and clerical tasks

1. Collecting money from pupils and parents.
2. Investigating a pupil's absence.
3. Bulk photocopying.
4. Typing or making word-processed versions of manuscript material and producing revisions of such versions.
5. Word-processing, copying and distributing bulk communications, including standard letters, to parents and pupils.
6. Producing class lists on the basis of information provided by teachers.
7. Keeping and filing records, including records based on data supplied by teachers.
8. Preparing, setting up and taking down classroom displays in accordance with decisions taken by teachers.
9. Producing analyses of attendance figures.
10. Producing analyses of examination results.
11. Collating pupil reports.
12. Administration of work experience (but not selecting placements and supporting pupils by advice or visits).
13. Administration of public and internal examinations.
14. Administration of cover for absent teachers.
15. Ordering, setting up and maintaining ICT equipment and software.
16. Ordering supplies and equipment.
17. Cataloguing, preparing, issuing and maintaining materials and equipment and stocktaking the same.
18. Taking verbatim notes or producing formal minutes of meetings.

19. Co-ordinating and submitting bids (for funding, school status and the like) using contributions by teachers and others.

20. Transferring manual data about pupils not covered by the above into computerised school management systems.

21. Managing the data in school management systems.

ANNEX 4 – Changes taking effect from 1st September 2009

1. Delete paragraph 19.3.2.

2. For paragraph 20.4, substitute-

"20.4 The application must contain-

(a) in the case where the teacher is subject to the 2006 Regulations and has had two or more reviews under those Regulations, a statement that he wishes to be considered for assessment against the post-threshold teacher standards;

(b) in the case where the teacher is subject to the 2006 Regulations and has had only one review under those Regulations, a statement that he wishes to be considered for assessment against the post-threshold teacher standards and a summary of evidence relating to that part of the relevant period not covered by the review which the teacher wishes to rely on in order to demonstrate that he has met the post-threshold teacher standards throughout the relevant period;

(c) in any other case, a statement that the teacher wishes to be considered for assessment against the post-threshold teacher standards and a summary of the evidence he wishes to rely on in order to demonstrate that he has met the post-threshold teacher standards throughout the relevant period.".

3. For paragraph 20.8, substitute-

"20.8 When carrying out the assessment against the post-threshold teacher standards the person to whom the task has been delegated must have regard only to-

(a) in the case where the teacher is subject to the 2006 Regulations and-

(i) has had two or more reviews under those Regulations, the results of the last two reviews;

(ii) has had only one review under those Regulations, the results of that review and the evidence mentioned in the application;

(b) in the case where the teacher is subject to the 2002 Regulations, the results of the most recent appraisal under the 2002 Regulations and the evidence mentioned in the application;

(c) in any other case, the evidence mentioned in the application.".

4. In paragraph 37-

(a) for sub-paragraph 5, including the heading, substitute-

37.5 **"Re-appointment of unqualified teachers**
In the case of a person previously employed as an unqualified teacher who is re-appointed with effect from 1st September 2009 or thereafter who has not previously been assimilated on to the new pay scale under sub-paragraph 7, the relevant body must determine the point above point 1 on the previous pay scale on which that teacher is to be placed in accordance with sub-paragraph 6; and if an unqualified teacher is not entitled to any points under that sub-paragraph he must be placed at point 1 on that pay scale.";

(b) for sub-paragraph 11, substitute-

"37.11 The relevant body may award an unqualified teacher-

(a) 1 point where he has been notified that a year of employment has not been satisfactory in respect of that year;

(b) 1 or more points for years of experience other than employment as an unqualified teacher which the relevant body considers to be of value to the performance of the unqualified teacher's duties;

(c) in a case to which paragraph 4.1(a) applies-

(i) where the teacher is not subject to the 2002 Regulations or the 2006 Regulations, his performance in the previous school year was excellent, having regard to all aspects of his professional duties, in particular, classroom teaching; or

(ii) where the teacher is subject to the 2002 Regulations or the 2006 Regulations, his performance in the previous school year was excellent, having regard to the results of the most recent appraisal carried out in accordance with the 2002 Regulations or the most recent review carried out in accordance with the 2006 Regulations, as the case may be;

(d) in the case of a teacher who was not employed as an unqualified teacher between 1st September 2005 and 31st August 2008, 1 point for each year of employment completed as an unqualified teacher prior to 1st September 2005."; and

(c) for sub-paragraph 15, substitute-

"37.15 The relevant body must award an unqualified teacher 1 point for each year of employment (interpreted in accordance with paragraph 1.8) completed as an unqualified teacher since 1st September 2008, unless he has been notified in accordance with sub-paragraph 10 that his service was unsatisfactory in respect of that year.

37.16 Any points awarded under this paragraph are permanent whether the unqualified teacher remains in the same post or takes up a new one.".

SECTION 3: Guidance on School Teachers' Pay and Conditions (general)

1. The guidance in this section, which relates to general pay matters, and the guidance on the National Agreement (Section 4) should be read in conjunction with any related paragraphs of the School Teachers' Pay and Conditions Document 2008 ('the Document'), and overall in relation to paragraph 1.9 of the Document which explains the basis on which local authorities ('LAs'), governing bodies and others must have regard to the guidance. Under paragraph 127 of the 2002 Education Act, LAs and governing bodies must have regard to guidance issued by the Secretary of State about the procedure to be followed in applying the provisions of the Document. A court or tribunal may take any failure of an employer to do so into account in any proceedings.

2. Paragraph references in this guidance relate, except where otherwise stated, to paragraph numbers in the Document. The term 'relevant body' denotes the body (either governing body or LA) which is responsible for pay decisions.

3. This guidance has been agreed by the Rewards and Incentives Group, as described in paragraph 6 of Section 1.

General principles

4. No payments or conditions of employment other than those provided for in the Document may be applied to teachers, except those conditions which are always determined locally and which do not conflict with the Document, unless the Secretary of State has granted exemptions under other legislation. The Document does not provide for the payment of so-called 'honoraria' in any circumstances.

5. A teacher's working week does not include Saturdays, Sundays or Public Holidays, unless his or her contract expressly provides for this (such as in the case of teachers at residential establishments). This is specified in paragraphs 64, 67, 72 and 77.2.

Pay policy and grievance procedures (paragraph 3)

Pay policy

6. All relevant bodies - both governing bodies and LAs where they are the relevant body, including for all unattached teachers - must have

a pay policy. This should be linked to the performance management[1] system. It should be reviewed annually and be kept up to date to take into account any legal changes or changes in the staffing structure which have an impact on discretionary pay decisions. Teachers and representatives of recognised unions should always be consulted on formulating the policy and on any changes to it. Teachers should always have ready access to copies of the relevant body's pay policy. Relevant bodies should be aware of the model pay policy which is available at www.teachernet.gov.uk/pay.

7. The Education (School Teacher Performance Management) (England) Regulations 2006 came into force on 1st September 2007. The revised performance management arrangements introduced by those Regulations affect pay decisions implemented after 31st August 2008, so relevant bodies should amend their pay policy in the light of these new arrangements with effect from 1st September 2008. The revised performance management arrangements do not apply to Wales.

8. The School Teachers' Appraisal Regulations 2002 ("the 2002 Regulations") apply to teachers in Wales. The Regulations provide for the appraisal of the performance of school teachers (including unqualified teachers) at maintained schools in Wales with the exception of those employed in non-standard settings, those teachers on contracts of less than a year, centrally employed teachers, teachers at pupil referral units, nursery school teachers and peripatetic teachers. For teachers in Wales who are not covered by the 2002 Regulations, relevant bodies should ensure that they review the performance of teachers on an annual basis where applicable for pay progression purposes.

9. The Freedom of Information Act 2000 requires all public authorities to make information available proactively through their publication scheme. LAs and governing bodies should consider whether pay policies should be included in their publication schemes, having regard to the public interest in allowing public access to information, as required by the Act. They must, under the Act, make copies available on demand.

1 There should be a transparent and fair process in place to ensure that the outcomes of performance management are used to inform pay decisions. Further information and guidance is available for England at http://www.teachernet.gov.uk/performancemanagement/ and for Wales at http://new.wales.gov.uk/topics/educationandskills/publications/guidance_and_information/performance-man-for-teachers?lang=en.

10. Procedures for determining pay must comply with all the requirements of discrimination legislation. The pay policy should therefore, make clear the relevant body's compliance with the following legislation, as amended: the Race Relations Act 1976, the Sex Discrimination Acts 1975 and 1986, the Equal Pay Act 1970, the Employment Relations Act 1999, the Disability Discrimination Act 1995, the Part-Time Worker (Prevention of Less Favourable Treatment) Regulations 2000, the Fixed-Term Employees (Prevention of Less Favourable Treatment) Regulations 2002, the Employment Equality (Sexual Orientation) Regulations 2003, the Employment Equality (Religion or Belief) Regulations 2003 and the Employment Equality (Age) Regulations 2006. Procedures for determining pay should also be consistent with the principles of public life - objectivity, openness and accountability.

11. The pay policy should set out how all pay decisions are made, either as part of a regular review or in other circumstances, with sufficient detail for an individual to appreciate what evidence and other factors will be taken into consideration when a pay decision is made. In particular, the pay policy should describe the information to be included on pay statements given to teachers as part of the regular review process, or when other pay decisions are taken, and how additional information may be obtained by teachers. Relevant bodies should be aware of the model pay statements which are available at www.teachernet.gov.uk/pay.

12. Where decisions relate to pay reviews, the policy must also specify the date by which such decisions must be made (see also paragraph 19 below). The policy should also take account of special circumstances such as absence on maternity or long-term sick leave, and the relevant body's approach to covering such situations in respect of the timing of pay reviews.

13. The pay policy should set out the principles by which the relevant body will exercise its discretion in pay matters. The relevant body should ensure that the effects of the application of those principles are reasonable in each case.

14. Relevant bodies should keep their staffing structure under review. The pay policy should be revised in accordance with decisions taken from time to time, following consultation, in relation to the staffing structure, and a copy of the structure and implementation plan (required under the Education (Review of Staffing Structure) (England) Regulations 2005 and the Education (Review of Staffing

Structure) (Wales) Regulations 2005) should be attached to the published copy of the pay policy. It is particularly important that the pay policy sets out the value of any Teaching and Learning Responsibility (TLR) payments attached to posts included in the staffing structure. Relevant bodies should ensure that all posts to which TLRs are attached meet the criteria for the award of TLRs (see paragraphs 63–70 below), that the cash value is determined by the particular responsibilities required by each such post and that equal pay legislation is respected.

Pay hearings and appeals

15. The pay policy must also set out the procedures that apply when any teacher seeks a review of any decision made by the head teacher or relevant body that affects his or her pay. A hearing and appeals procedure is included in the model pay policy at www.teachernet.gov.uk/pay. Hearings and appeals against pay decisions must meet the dispute resolution requirements of employment law, in accordance with section 29 of, and Schedule 2 to, the Employment Rights Act 2002 (further information is at www.berr.gov.uk/employment/Resolving disputes/index.html).

16. Any teacher seeking a reconsideration of a pay decision should first seek to resolve the matter informally through discussion with the decision-maker within 10 working days of notification of the decision. Where this is not possible, or the matter is still unresolved, the teacher may follow the formal grievance process by setting out their concerns in writing to the decision-maker within 10 working days of the notification of the decision or the outcome of the informal discussion.

17. The committee or person who made the decision should provide a hearing within 10 working days to consider the teacher's concerns. The teacher should be informed in writing of the decision and the right to appeal. Any appeal against the decision of the hearing should be heard by a panel of three governors who were not involved in the original determination, normally within 20 working days of the written appeal notification. The teacher should be given the opportunity to make representations in person at both the hearing and the appeal and to be accompanied by a friend or union representative (www.berr.gov.uk/employment/trade-union-rights/trade-unions/grievance-hearings/page16831.html). The decision of the appeal panel should be given in writing, and where the appeal is rejected include a note of the evidence considered and the reasons for the decision.

18. The pay hearings and appeals procedure performs the function of the grievance procedure on pay matters and therefore decisions should not be reopened under general grievance procedures. Appeal decisions do not affect teachers' statutory employment rights.

Timing of salary determination and notification (paragraph 4)

19. Relevant bodies should conduct teachers' annual pay reviews without undue delay. The pay policy should set out the date by which decisions (effective from 1 September each year) will be made (see paragraph 12 above), which should be by 31 October at latest, except in the case of head teachers for whom the deadline is 31 December. However, where decisions are actually made earlier than the date set, these should be notified to the teacher at the earliest opportunity.

20. Where a review of the staffing structure has had, or is likely to have, an impact on the pay of any teacher, a revised pay statement should be issued as soon as possible (and in any event within one month of the relevant body's determination). Relevant bodies should take particular care to notify teachers of likely changes to their pay at the earliest opportunity because teachers must be informed of any pay safeguarding implications resulting from the revisions. Relevant bodies should ensure that teachers are given full information about the safeguarding rules with the revised pay statement, to enable teachers to calculate the likely longer-term position in relation to their own pay. (A guidance note on the rules is at www.teachernet.gov.uk/pay.)

Teachers paid a safeguarded sum (paragraph 5)

21. The relevant body must review the duties of any teachers who are entitled to safeguarded sums that in total exceed £500 (excluding generally safeguarded recruitment and retention payments) and allocate appropriate additional responsibilities, commensurate with the safeguarded sum, for the period of safeguarding (see paragraph 5.1). The relevant body should ensure that appropriate notice is given of any new duties which are being given to the teacher as work commensurate with their safeguarded sum or sums. All such additional responsibilities allocated should be kept under review, including taking such action as may be required when the safeguarding period ends. Head teachers will want to consider

whether the additional duty is still required; if it should now attract an additional payment (such as a TLR payment); and, if so, the most appropriate person to undertake the duty.

22. The relevant body should ensure that all teachers who are, or will be, in receipt of safeguarded sums are aware, that if they unreasonably refuse to carry out such additional duties, payment of the safeguarded sums will cease. The teacher must be given written notice of any determination to withdraw a safeguarded sum at least one month before it is implemented and should be given notice of such a determination at the earliest opportunity. Any such determination is subject to appeal in the usual way.

23. Relevant bodies should be aware of the general principle set out in paragraph 5.2. This requires the relevant body to consider whether a teacher's new pay point or new allowance has caused the teacher's pay to increase by as much as or more than the value of their previous point and any safeguarded sum they were receiving. (Changes in the value of allowances or of pay points which result from the provisions of the Document are excluded[2].) If a range of safeguarded elements is being paid, 'safeguarded sum' does not mean the total of all safeguarded elements, but any safeguarded element within the total. The safeguarding guidance at www.teachernet.gov.uk/pay gives further information.

24. Where any such increase is larger than any safeguarded sum, the relevant body must cease to pay any sum or sums equal to or less than the increase. If there is a decision needed as to which sum or sums to cease paying, the relevant body should always cease paying the smaller or smallest sum first, followed by the next smallest, at any time when necessary to ensure that the principle is correctly applied.

25. Relevant bodies should note that paragraph 5.3 sets out the provisions for determining the latest end date for safeguarding of TLRs, the unqualified teachers' allowance and for members of the leadership group, ASTs and excellent teachers who are subject to safeguarding under paragraph 47. In such cases, safeguarding ends on the third anniversary of one of three set dates, in accordance with when the relevant body make their determination (see safeguarding guidance at www.teachernet/gov.uk/pay for more information).

2 Generally this means increases resulting from pay awards following recommendations of the School Teachers' Review Body.

SECTION 3

Leadership Group Pay (paragraphs 6-16)

Individual school range

26. Relevant bodies should assign a school to a head teacher group and determine the individual school range (ISR) whenever they propose to appoint a new head teacher. They should also re-determine the ISR if they change the head teacher group in any other circumstances or if they set a deputy or assistant head teacher pay range which overlaps with the ISR. They may determine the ISR as of 1 September 2008 or at any time if they consider it necessary to retain a head teacher.

27. When determining the ISR, within the permitted parameters set out in paragraph 12, the relevant body should take account of any difficulties there may be in recruiting and retaining a head teacher and whether there has been a significant change in the responsibilities of the head teacher. The relevant body should not take account of the salary of the serving head teacher if they re-determine the ISR.

28. When determining the actual salary of a new head teacher, relevant bodies should take account of the responsibilities of the post, the background of the pupils at the school and whether the post is difficult to fill.

29. The relevant body should determine the pay range for deputies and assistant heads when they propose to make new appointments or where there is a significant change in the responsibilities of serving deputy or assistant heads. They should take account of the responsibilities of the post, the background of the pupils at the school and whether the post is difficult to fill. They may determine the pay range as of 1 September 2008 or at any time if they consider it necessary to retain a deputy or assistant head teacher.

30. Relevant bodies should ensure that they review the performance of members of the leadership group, where they are not subject to the 2002 Regulations or the 2006 Regulations[3], in accordance with paragraphs 7, 13 or 15 as applicable. For all teachers, relevant bodies should take full account of the clarification of the application of the criteria for leadership group progression set out in the following box, in the light of any considerations set out in the relevant body's own pay policy as referred to in paragraphs 11–13 above. For teachers in England who are subject to the 2006 Regulations, relevant bodies must have regard to any recommendation on pay progression recorded in the teacher's most recent planning and review statement.

3 This means any teachers who are not subject to performance management.

Application of Leadership Group Pay Progression Criteria – Clarification

Those on the leadership spine play a critical role in the life of the school. They inspire confidence in those around them and work with others to create a shared strategic vision which motivates pupils and staff. They take the lead in enhancing standards of teaching and learning and value enthusiasm and innovation in others. They have the confidence and ability to make management and organisational decisions and ensure equity, access and entitlement to learning.

To achieve progression, the School Teachers' Pay and Conditions Document (STPCD) requires individuals on the leadership spine to have demonstrated sustained high quality performance. To be fair and transparent, judgements must be properly rooted in evidence and there must have been a successful review of overall performance.

A successful performance review, as prescribed by the Regulations[4], will involve a performance management process of:

- performance objectives;
- classroom observation (where relevant);
- other evidence.

To ensure that there has been high quality performance, the performance review will need to assess that the teacher has grown professionally by developing their leadership and (where relevant) teaching expertise.

SECTION 3

Pay scale for classroom teachers (paragraph 17)

31. The relevant body may award an additional point to any main scale teacher whose performance in the previous school year was excellent, with particular regard to classroom teaching. Where the teacher is subject to the 2002 Regulations (in Wales) or the 2006 Regulations (in England), this decision will follow the most recent appraisal/review[5]. For teachers in England who are subject to the 2006 Regulations, relevant bodies must have regard to any recommendation on pay progression recorded in the teacher's most recent planning and review statement. The provisions for main scale progression under paragraph 18.1.1(b) remain unchanged.

4 The Education (School Teacher Performance Management) (England) Regulations 2006, and The Education (School Teacher Appraisal) (Wales) Regulations 2002.

5 This means any teachers who are not subject to performance management.

SECTION 3

Review of the salary of post-threshold teachers (paragraph 19)

32. For those teachers not subject to the 2002 Regulations or the 2006 Regulations[6], relevant bodies should ensure that they review the performance of post-threshold teachers who are eligible for consideration for movement up the upper pay scale in accordance with the criteria in paragraph 19. For those teachers subject to the 2002 Regulations or the 2006 Regulations, when considering whether the teacher meets the criteria in paragraph 19 the relevant body must have regard to the results of the two most recent appraisals or reviews carried out in accordance with the 2001 Regulations, the 2002 Regulations or the 2006 Regulations. For all teachers relevant bodies should take full account of the clarification of the application of the criteria for upper pay scale progression set out in the following box, in the light of any considerations set out in the relevant body's own pay policy as referred to in paragraphs 11–13 above. Where teachers have moved school in the assessment period, the head teacher should consult with the head of the teacher's previous school to seek evidence as to the teacher's suitability for progression.

33. Relevant bodies have discretion under paragraph 19.3.3 to determine the point on the upper pay scale to which certain categories of post-threshold teachers may be appointed. When doing so, relevant bodies should consider any pay progression which such teachers made in their previous employment which was based on an assessment of standards and contribution comparable to the requirements for progression on the upper pay scale; and should not unreasonably withhold appointment at the equivalent point on the upper pay scale.

Changes to pay determination arrangements from 1 September 2009 (Annex 4)

34. Annex 4 removes the provision, as set out in paragraph 19.3.2 of the STPCD 2007, for backdating the salary award to 1 September in the school year in which the teacher made his application. From 1 September 2009, a successful threshold application will result in the teacher moving to point U1 of the pay scale for post-threshold teachers with effect from 1 September in the following school year.

35. This means that any teacher currently paid on point M6 of the pay scale for classroom teachers for a year or more and who has either

6 This means any teachers who are not subject to performance management.

(a) never applied for threshold assessment or (b) applied and been unsuccessful, will need to make a successful application between 1 September 2008 and 31 August 2009 (Round 9) in order to be paid on point U1 with effect from 1 September 2008.

Application of Upper Pay Scale Progression Criteria – Clarification

U3 teachers play a critical role in the life of the school. They provide a role model for teaching and learning, make a distinctive contribution to the raising of pupil standards and contribute effectively to the work of the wider team. They take advantage of appropriate opportunities for professional development and use the outcomes effectively to improve pupils' learning.

The following paragraphs refer to all teachers seeking to progress on the Upper Pay Scale.

To achieve progression, the School Teachers' Pay and Conditions Document (STPCD) requires that the achievements of post-threshold teachers and their contribution to school(s) should have been substantial and sustained. To be fair and transparent, judgements must be properly rooted in evidence and there must have been a successful review of overall performance.

Progression on UPS should be based on two successful consecutive performance management reviews, other than under the exceptional circumstances as set out in the STPCD.

A successful performance review as prescribed by the Regulations[7] involves a performance management process of

- performance objectives;
- classroom observation;
- other evidence.

To ensure that the achievements and contribution have been substantial and sustained, that performance review will need to assess that the teacher has:

- continued to meet post-threshold standards; and
- grown professionally by developing their teaching expertise post threshold.

7 See footnote 5.

Assessment against the post-threshold standards (paragraph 20)

Role of the relevant body in assessment against the post-threshold standards

36. The relevant body has legal responsibility for the threshold process. However, it is required to delegate the receipt and assessment of applications to the head teacher (or person with management responsibility in the case of unattached teachers). That person should handle all practical aspects of the process, including the giving of feedback to applicants.

37. The head teacher (or person with management responsibility in the case of unattached teachers) should promptly notify the relevant body of his or her decision on the application when it has been assessed. The relevant body, on receiving notification of a successful threshold application, is under a duty to move the teacher concerned to U1 in accordance with paragraph 19 of the Document. For guidance and an explanatory table on payment dates, relevant bodies should refer to the *Threshold Assessment 2008/09, Round 9 Guidance* (http://www.teachernet.gov.uk/management/payandperformance/threshold/).

Professional standards for teachers in England

38. The standards for post-threshold teachers are set out in Annex 1 to the Document. In England, these standards are part of a framework of professional standards which is intended to help teachers as they plan their careers and discuss their future development with their line managers. The standards provide a backdrop to discussions about how a teacher's performance should be viewed in relation to their current career stage and the career stage they are approaching.

39. Within the framework, the standards are designed to be cumulative and progressive. The core standards underpin all the subsequent standards and continue to apply at all subsequent career stages. Each set of standards builds on the previous set, so that a teacher being assessed against the post-threshold standards must also meet the core standards. Where teachers are subject to performance management, assessment that a teacher meets the core standards is carried out through the performance management process.

Standards for teachers in Wales

40. The standards framework as a whole, as set out in Annex 1, applies in England only. The standards for post-threshold teachers, Excellent Teachers and ASTs set out in Annex 1 are pay standards and apply in England and Wales. Responsibility for setting non-pay standards rests with the Welsh Assembly Government.

Applications, evidence period and absence

41. Assessment is a voluntary process and entirely a matter of choice for individuals. Teachers are responsible for applying for assessment and they must apply to the head teacher of the school or setting at which they are employed to teach (or head of service if applicable). An application form is available through TeacherNet at http://www.teachernet.gov.uk/management/payandperformance/threshold/

42. It is the teacher's responsibility to provide summarised evidence – in the form of concrete examples from their day-to-day work – in support of an application. This evidence should be as recent as possible and clearly demonstrate that the teacher has worked at the level indicated by the post-threshold standards for a sustained period immediately before the application is submitted. Normally, the evidence should cover the two years leading up to and ending at the date of their application. In certain circumstances (see paragraph 43 below), evidence collated over a period of up to five years can be taken into account. The evidence of teaching should be taken from all educational settings where the applicant has taught children of school age (up to 19 years of age). A year for the purposes of evidence for post-threshold standards is defined in paragraph 1.8 of the Document and it permits certain periods of absence to be counted towards the period of a year.

43. Teachers who have not been teaching children up to 19 years of age in the two years immediately preceding their application and who are not covered by the specific absences defined in paragraph 1.8 of the Document, or where the relevant body does not exercise its discretion to recognise the absence, but who have worked for an aggregate period of at least two years in the five years preceding their application, should cite evidence from the most recent two year period (or an aggregate) ending at the point when they last taught children up to 19 years of age. They should not cite evidence more than five years old.

44. The absences not covered by paragraph 1.8 of the Document could be as a result of the teacher being an individual who had taught entirely outside the maintained or school sector, as a result of secondment, study leave, or because they took a career break for reasons other than those specifically covered by paragraph 1.8 and regardless of whether the break was in-service or not.

Feedback

All teachers - returning the application form and oral feedback

45. Before the head teacher assesses whether the teacher meets the post-threshold standards as set out in Annex 1 of the Document, he or she must first be satisfied, through the outcomes of performance reviews, that the teacher meets the core standards set out in Annex 1.

46. If the head teacher is satisfied, through the outcomes of performance reviews, that the teacher meets the core standards, he or she must go on to assess whether the teacher meets the post-threshold standards.

47. If the head teacher is not satisfied, through the outcomes of performance reviews, that the teacher meets the core standards he or she must reject the application and provide the teacher with a written explanation for the rejection. He or she should do this within 20 working days of informing the relevant body of the decision. In such cases, no assessment will be carried out against the post-threshold standards.

48. Having carried out an assessment against the post-threshold standards, the head teacher must notify the teacher of the outcome of that assessment and should do this within 20 working days of informing the relevant body of the decision. He or she should also return the teacher's application form to him or her, showing any findings/comments he or she may have recorded on that form.

49. The head teacher should provide oral feedback on each of the 10 post-threshold standards and the reasons for the outcome of the application.

50. Feedback should be sensitive, informative and developmental. Feedback should link effectively to the school's performance management arrangements and should enable the teacher and his/her manager to identify clear priorities for future professional development.

Unsuccessful applicants

51. In the case of unsuccessful applicants, head teachers should give written feedback on the reasons for the outcome of the application, in relation to each of the 10 post-threshold standards, including those where the standards have been met, within 20 working days of informing the relevant body of their decision.

52. Heads should record their reasons for determining that the standard(s) have not yet been met. A record of the concise reasons for which standard has/has not been met and why, should provide sufficient written feedback, although the head may supplement this. In all cases, the aim should be to give clear advice in oral feedback about how the teacher needs to develop in order to reach the standards. If, in discussion with the teacher it has been necessary to amplify the comments, then the key additional points made should be confirmed in writing.

Appeals against not meeting the post-threshold standards

53. Paragraphs 15 - 18 above, which cover hearings and appeals in connection with pay determinations, also apply to decisions with regard to post-threshold standards.

Teachers who have worked in two or more schools during the evidence period

54. Teachers who cite evidence from more than one school (e.g. supply teachers who have had specific individual contracts with schools and therefore were attached to those schools, or teachers who have changed jobs) should submit their application to the relevant body of the school they are contracted to work in on the date of submission of their application.

55. That head teacher should consult with the heads of the other schools in assessing the application and those heads should participate in the assessment.

Teachers who work in two or more schools simultaneously

56. In exceptional circumstances, where a post-threshold applicant is simultaneously employed to teach at two or more schools (e.g. part-time teachers simultaneously employed in two or more schools, or supply teachers simultaneously employed in two or more schools

and attached to those schools) the teacher should submit their application to the head teacher of the school at which they spend most time and the head of that school should normally assess the application, with appropriate input from the heads of the other school or schools. Where the teacher spends equal time in every school, they should submit their application to the head teacher of the school at which they have been employed the longest and the head of that school should normally be responsible for making the assessment. The assessing head should consult with the other head teachers in assessing the application and they should participate in the assessment. Where all the relevant heads agree, it is also possible for any one of them to assess the application if appropriate.

57. Teachers may make only one application, however many schools they work in. Regardless of the number of heads who contribute to the assessment, only one head should decide whether each of the standards has been met.

Changes to application and assessment arrangements for teachers in England from September 2009 (Annex 4)

58. Annex 4 specifies the changes to the threshold application and assessment process in England which will be effective from 1 September 2009.

   a. A teacher applying for assessment who is subject to the 2006 Regulations and who has had two or more reviews under those Regulations will be assessed against the post-threshold standards based solely on the contents of the last two planning and review statements. No other evidence may be taken into account.

   b. A teacher applying for assessment who is subject to the 2006 Regulations and who has had only one review under those Regulations will be assessed against the post-threshold standards based on the contents of that planning and review statement and the evidence in their application.

   c. A teacher applying for assessment who is subject to the 2002 Regulations will be assessed against the post-threshold standards based on the evidence in their application and with regard to the results of their most recent appraisal.

59. A teacher applying for assessment who is not subject to the 2002 Regulations or the 2006 Regulations will continue to be assessed against the post-threshold standards based on the evidence in their application.

Allowances for classroom teachers

Safeguarding management allowances (paragraph 21)

60. Management allowances ceased to be available from 1 January 2006. Former management allowances are subject to the rules on safeguarding set out in paragraph 21 (see www.teachernet.gov.uk/pay for rules). The safeguarding of all management allowances expires by 31 December 2008 at the latest and cannot be extended[8]. Fixed-period management allowances are safeguarded for no longer than the length of the fixed period originally set.

61. Relevant bodies should take account of the expiry dates of management allowances and be clear how any TLRs will be introduced alongside management allowances still being paid on a safeguarded basis.

62. If a teacher in receipt of management allowance safeguarding is awarded a TLR in the temporary absence of the postholder, or serves as a member of the leadership group, as an advanced skills teacher or as an excellent teacher in the temporary absence of the postholder, management allowance safeguarding is reduced or discontinued (as applicable) during this period but is restored at the end of the temporary period unless it would otherwise have ceased under the provisions of paragraph 21.

Teaching and Learning Responsibility payments (paragraphs 22 - 25)

63. TLRs may be awarded for undertaking a sustained responsibility in the context of the school's staffing structure that is needed to ensure continued delivery of high-quality teaching and learning. Posts to which TLRs are attached must meet the criterion and factors which are set out in paragraph 22 of the Document and summarised in the box below. The monetary values of TLRs must also be determined within the parameters in paragraph 22 and set out below.

8 Different arrangements apply to management allowances safeguarded under former general safeguarding arrangements – see paragraph 46 of the Document and paragraphs 124-125 below.

64. The relevant body must keep under review how many leadership group posts, advanced skills teacher, excellent teacher and other posts are needed in its staffing structure and whether TLRs are an appropriate part of the structure needed to ensure the continued delivery of high-quality teaching and learning[9]. If TLRs are an appropriate part of that structure, the relevant body must decide how many posts should have TLRs and the appropriate cash values (uprated in accordance with paragraphs 23 and 24), in the light of the criterion and factors for the award of TLR2 and TLR1 and the parameters within which the cash values may be set. The responsibility or package of responsibilities for which a TLR is awarded should be clearly set out in the job description of the post holder. Equal pay legislation must be respected in the award of TLRs to individual teachers and relevant bodies should be aware that any decisions which are not made on objective criteria may lead to claims being made to employment tribunals.

65. Teachers are expected to contribute, both orally and in writing as appropriate, to curriculum development by sharing their professional expertise with colleagues and advising on effective practice. This does not mean that they can be expected to take on the responsibility of, and accountability for, a subject area or to manage other teachers without appropriate additional payment. Responsibilities of this nature should be part of a post that is in the leadership group or linked to a post which attracts a TLR on the basis set out in paragraph 22.

CRITERION AND FACTORS FOR THE AWARD OF TEACHING AND LEARNING RESPONSIBILITY PAYMENTS, AND VALUES

Criterion

A Teaching and Learning Responsibility payment ("TLR") may be awarded to a classroom teacher for undertaking a sustained additional responsibility in the context of the relevant body's staffing structure for the purpose of ensuring the continued delivery of high-quality teaching and learning and for which he is made accountable. The award may be while the teacher remains in the same post or occupies another post in the temporary absence of the post-holder.

9 If a post meets the criterion and all of the factors, this does not mean automatically that the post will be graded as a TLR1. In addition, in some schools, the structure may provide for the leadership group to carry out some or all of the associated responsibilities.

Factors

Before awarding a TLR, the relevant body must be satisfied that the teacher's duties include a significant responsibility that is not required of all classroom teachers, and that -

- is focused on teaching and learning;
- requires the exercise of a teacher's professional skills and judgement;
- requires the teacher to lead, manage and develop a subject or curriculum area; or to lead and manage pupil development across the curriculum;
- has an impact on the educational progress of pupils other than the teacher's assigned classes or groups of pupils; and
- involves leading, developing and enhancing the teaching practice of other staff.

Before awarding a TLR1, the relevant body must be satisfied that the significant responsibility referred to in the previous paragraph includes in addition line management responsibility for a significant number of people.

Values

Having decided to award a TLR, the relevant body must determine whether to award a TLR1 or a TLR2 and its value, in accordance with its pay policy, provided that-

- the annual value of a TLR1 shall be no less than £6,997 and no greater than £11,841;
- the annual value of a TLR2 shall be no less than £2,422 and no greater than £5,920; and
- if the relevant body awards TLRs of different values to two or more teachers, the minimum difference in value between each award of a TLR1 is £1,500; and between each award of a TLR2 is £1,500.

66. Relevant bodies should determine the value of a TLR appropriate for the post, within the parameters laid down and in accordance with job weight. Posts of equal weight should be allocated equal value. Decisions to make payments above the applicable minimum level

should be justifiable in relation to the level of responsibilities attached to the post. Relevant bodies should not take into account recruitment or retention issues, payments for which should only be awarded under the provisions of paragraph 53 and in accordance with the relevant body's pay policy. Changes in the value of TLRs, once set by the relevant body, should only occur for two reasons: (a) the STRB recommends, and the Secretary of State accepts and brings in a general change in the TLR values[10]; or (b) the relevant body reviews its staffing structure and determines that the responsibilities of the post have changed materially.

67. Relevant bodies should operate in line with their reviewed staffing structure and implementation plan to introduce TLRs, as applicable, by 31 December 2008. They should award TLRs to teachers placed in the specified posts in the staffing structure and to the cash value set out in the pay policy, uprated in accordance with paragraphs 23 and 24 of the Document. TLRs awarded to part-time teachers must be paid pro-rata at the same proportion as the teacher's part-time contract.

68. TLRs are permanent while the postholder remains in the same post in the staffing structure. A teacher may not be awarded more than one TLR. The overarching criterion for the award of TLRs includes provisions that the responsibility for which the TLR is awarded must be 'sustained' and that the TLR must be awarded 'in the context of the relevant body's staffing structure'. TLRs may only be awarded on a temporary basis where the teacher is temporarily occupying a different post in the staffing structure to which a TLR payment is attached (such as in cases of cover for secondments, maternity or sick leave or vacancies pending permanent appointment) and for the duration of that responsibility. TLRs may not be awarded in any other circumstances, for example where the responsibility is short-term or fixed-term, because such circumstances would not meet the overarching criterion, as outlined above, for the award of TLRs. The date on which the temporary award will end, or the circumstances in which it will end, must be included in the teacher's notice of a revised pay determination, as specified in paragraph 4.4(c)(iii) of the Document. A teacher who holds a TLR awarded on a temporary basis or who is on a fixed-term contract does not receive a safeguarded sum when the TLR comes to an end, unless the TLR is ended earlier than specified and their contract extends beyond the date when that TLR ends.

10 From 1 September 2008 all TLRs in payment must be uprated by 2.45%, and those not yet in payment but set out in the staffing structure must be similarly uprated. This does not affect any management allowance safeguarding.

69. If a teacher is given a new post or revised responsibilities, then the relevant body must determine whether a different TLR (or no TLR) applies to the post, and whether the teacher is entitled to any safeguarded sum if no TLR, or a lower one, applies to the new post/revised responsibilities.

70. If a teacher in receipt of TLR safeguarding is awarded a TLR in the temporary absence of the postholder, or serves as a member of the leadership group, as an advanced skills teacher or as an excellent teacher in the temporary absence of the postholder, TLR safeguarding is reduced or discontinued (as applicable) during this period but is restored at the end of the temporary period unless it would otherwise have ceased under the provisions of paragraph 25.

Special educational needs allowance (paragraph 26)

71. SEN allowances may be held at the same time as TLRs. However, relevant bodies should, when keeping their staffing structures under review:

- ensure that, in the light of remodelling and the move of administrative tasks from teachers to support staff, holders of discretionary SEN allowances are not carrying out tasks that would be more appropriately undertaken by support staff;
- consider whether, if teachers have responsibilities that meet all the criteria for the award of TLR payments it would not be more appropriate to award a TLR payment *instead of* a discretionary SEN allowance of a lower value;
- not continue to award new discretionary SEN payments solely for the purposes of recruitment and retention; and
- ensure that any SEN responsibilities are clearly specified in individual teachers' job descriptions, and are clear in the school's published staffing structure.

72. Where a discretionary SEN allowance is awarded, as well as specifying the level, the teacher's written notification given at the time of the award should specify the reason for the award.

73. Relevant bodies should ensure that their pay policies set out clearly the basis on which SEN2 should be awarded. When considering the award of SEN2, the relevant body should in particular consider what

relevant postgraduate qualifications or experience holders of SEN1 have, and whether these are being used for the benefit of the school or service. SEN2 should be awarded to all whose qualifications or experience are in line with the relevant body's policy.

Assimilation safeguarding (paragraph 27)

74. Relevant bodies should be aware of the arrangements regarding teachers subject to assimilation safeguarding. All sums payable under assimilation safeguarding arrangements as at 31 December 2005 are safeguarded on a cash basis for up to three years from 1 January 2006. All assimilation safeguarding ends by 31 December 2008. See paragraphs 21 – 24 above and www.teachernet.gov.uk/pay for further guidance.

Advanced Skills Teachers (paragraph 29)

SECTION 3

Setting pay ranges

75. When setting the pay range for an AST post (paragraph 29), in addition to the provisions in paragraph 29.3, relevant bodies should also consider the following:

- the status of the grade as an alternative to posts paid on the leadership spine;
- the need for an appropriately substantial pay increase in relation to the appointee's previous post;
- whether the post would or may otherwise have attracted an allowance (for example, for SEN);
- any recruitment or retention considerations; and
- whether the appointee is a teacher of a shortage subject or a subject where there is a particular need to raise the quality of teaching and learning.

76. The relevant body should determine the pay range for ASTs when they propose to make new appointments or where there is significant change in the responsibilities of existing ASTs, for example, higher-level responsibilities such as leading a large whole-school or LA project to improve an aspect of teaching and learning; or where there are changes in the school's situation which lead to a wider review of salaries.

Reviewing performance

77. Where the teacher is not subject to the 2002 Regulations or the 2006 Regulations[11], relevant bodies should ensure that they review the performance of ASTs who are eligible for consideration for movement up their pay range in accordance with paragraph 29. For those teachers subject to the 2002 Regulations or the 2006 Regulations the relevant body must have regard to the most recent appraisal or review when considering this. For those teachers subject to the 2006 Regulations, relevant bodies must have regard to any recommendation on pay progression recorded in the teacher's planning and review statement. For all teachers relevant bodies should take full account of the following notes on the clarification of the application of the criteria for advanced skills teacher pay progression, in the light of any considerations set out in the relevant body's own pay policy as referred to in paragraphs 11 – 13 above.

Application of Advanced Skills Teacher Pay Progression Criteria – Clarification

78. Advanced Skills Teachers play a critical role in the life of the school. Through their own excellent teaching and their work with other teachers or on whole school projects they play a leading role in enhancing the quality of teaching and learning throughout the school. Their outreach work opens the school to wider relationships which can enrich the experiences and raise the performance of both colleagues and pupils. Their outreach work also benefits and is of great value to the wider teaching community.

79. To achieve progression, the Document requires individuals on the advanced skills teacher spine to have demonstrated sustained high quality performance. To be fair and transparent, judgements must be properly rooted in evidence and there must have been a successful review of overall performance.

80. Such a performance management review must take place each year and a successful review can result in a movement of one or two points up the teacher's pay range.

11 That is, teachers in England and Wales not subject to performance management.

SECTION 3

81. A successful performance review as prescribed by the Regulations[12] will involve a performance management process of:

- performance objectives;
- classroom observation;
- other evidence.

82. To ensure that there has been high quality performance the performance review will need to assess that the teacher has grown professionally by developing their teaching expertise and their application and delivery of AST professional duties.

83. In order to take outreach work into account in determining whether there should be any movement up the AST pay spine (paragraph 29, relevant bodies should ensure that good systems are in place to monitor and evaluate this, particularly if it is organised and managed by someone outside the school, such as an LA AST co-ordinator.

Assessment against the AST or Excellent Teacher standards (paragraphs 32 and 33)

Revised professional standards for teachers in England

84. The standards for excellent teachers and ASTs are set out in Annex 1. For teachers in England these standards are part of a framework of professional standards which also contains standards for the award of QTS, standards for teachers on the main pay scale who have successfully completed their induction (the core standards) and standards for post-threshold teachers. Within the framework the standards are designed to be cumulative and progressive. As a result there are some standards which are only defined at one career stage but which continue to apply at all subsequent career stages. Teachers wishing to progress to a different career stage must also fulfil any relevant eligibility criteria, as well as meet the appropriate standards.

Standards for teachers in Wales

85. The standards for excellent teachers and ASTs are set out in Annex 1. The framework as a whole, as set out in section 1, applies in England only. The standards for excellent teachers and ASTs are pay standards and apply in England and Wales. Responsibility for setting non-pay standards rests with the Welsh Assembly Government.

12 See footnote 4.

Applications

86. The head teacher must first be satisfied that the teacher meets the standards which apply to his or her current level before he or she can be assessed against the AST and/or excellent teacher standards, as the case may be.

87. A teacher who does not already hold a certificate indicating that he or she meets the AST or excellent teacher standards should submit a written application for such a certificate to the head teacher of the school at which he or she is currently employed when he applies for an AST or excellent teacher post. In the case of excellent teacher posts, a teacher is only eligible to apply for a post in a school other than the one in which he or she is currently working if he has already been assessed as meeting the excellent teacher standards.

88. If he or she is simultaneously employed at more than one school the head teachers of the schools concerned should agree which one of them is to act as the designated head teacher to carry out the head teacher's duties under paragraph 60.11. If they cannot agree, then the designated head teacher should be either the head teacher of the school at which he or she is employed for the greatest number of hours or, if there is no difference, the head teacher of the school at which he or she has been employed for longest.

89. An unattached teacher should give his or her application to his or her line manager.

90. The head teacher should first be satisfied, by taking account of performance management reviews, that the teacher meets those standards set out in Annex 1 of the Document which apply to his or her current career stage.

91. Where the application is for an excellent teacher post, the standards which apply to his or her current career stage are the core and post-threshold standards.

92. Where the application is for an AST post, the standards which apply to his or her current career stage are:

   a. in the case of an applicant who is an Excellent Teacher, the core, post-threshold and excellent teacher standards;

   b. in the case of an applicant who is currently paid on the upper pay spine, the core and post-threshold standards;

c. in the case of an applicant who is currently paid on the main scale, the core standards.

93. If the head teacher is not satisfied that the teacher meets the standards which apply to his or her current career stage he or she must reject the application and provide the teacher with a written explanation for the rejection. He or she should do this within 20 working days of receiving the application. In such cases no external assessment will be carried out.

94. If the head teacher is satisfied that the teacher meets the standards which apply to his or her current career stage set out in Annex 1 he or she should complete the application within 20 working days of receiving it, adding his or her evaluation of the extent to which the teacher meets those standards set out in Annex 1 which are to be externally assessed as set out in the table below. He or she should give the teacher a copy of the completed application promptly.

Career Stage	Application for	External assessment against
Post-Threshold Teacher	Excellent Teacher	Excellent Teacher Standards
Main scale Teacher	Advanced Skills Teacher	Post-threshold, Excellent Teacher and Advanced Skills Teacher standards
Post-Threshold Teacher	Advanced Skills Teachers	Excellent Teacher and Advanced Skills Teacher standards
Excellent Teacher	Advanced Skills Teacher	Advanced Skills Teacher standards

95. Where the teacher is employed at more than one school, the designated head teacher should consult the head teachers of the other schools at which the teacher is employed before completing the application.

96. Where a teacher applies for an excellent teacher post at the school at which he or she is employed as a teacher, the head teacher should submit the completed application to an assessor.

97. Where an unattached teacher applies for an excellent teacher post at the LA at which he or she is employed, the relevant Chief Education Officer's nominee should submit the completed application to an assessor.

98. Where a teacher applies for an AST post at the school at which he or she is employed as a teacher, the head teacher should submit the completed application to an assessor if the teacher:

a. is selected for interview for the post; or

b. is selected, or recommended by the governing body, for appointment to the post without interview.

99. Where a teacher applies for an AST post at another school, the person who completed his or her application should give it to the head teacher of the school at which the post is situated. That head teacher should submit the completed application to an assessor in the above circumstances.

100. Where a teacher applies for an AST post which is not attached to a particular school, the person who completed his or her application should give it to the relevant Chief Education Officer's nominee. The nominee should submit the completed application to an assessor in the above circumstances.

Advanced Skills Teacher and Excellent Teacher Assessment

101. When making an assessment against the AST and excellent teacher standards an assessor should:

- consider the completed application;
- consider any additional evidence supplied by the applicant in support of his or her application;
- consider any additional evidence in relation to the application supplied by the head teacher or the applicant's line manager;
- observe the teacher teaching;
- interview him or her; and
- interview the head teacher or the applicant's line manager,

and he or she may seek such additional evidence as he or she sees fit to demonstrate those standards.

102. When an applicant is absent from work in the exercise of his or her statutory rights to maternity, paternity, adoption or parental leave, the assessor is not required to observe the teacher teaching.

Review of AST and Excellent Teacher assessment (paragraph 34)

103. An application for a review should be made in writing and submitted to the review co-ordinator appointed by the Secretary of State within 40 working days of receipt of the decision. It should contain or refer to evidence relating to the grounds upon which review is sought.

AST Outreach

104. ASTs working in schools in special measures, causing serious concern or facing challenging circumstances may use their outreach time to carry out AST professional duties in their own school.

105. In the following exceptional circumstances ASTs may vary the normal 20% of their time spent on outreach to a minimum of 10% and a maximum of 40% of their time on outreach work:

- where it is not possible to perform AST professional duties in relation to their own school at a time when the AST would normally be working in the school – for example because other staff are not available;
- where it is necessary to undertake AST professional developmental activities during time normally set aside for outreach work – for example because of the timing of external events and activities;
- when additional outreach work is undertaken in connection with a specific Departmental or National Assembly for Wales initiative; or
- where the AST is new and inexperienced.

Excellent Teachers (paragraph 35)

Determination of salary

106. The salary of any teacher appointed to an excellent teacher post on or after 1 September 2008 must be determined in accordance with sub-paragraphs 4 and 5.

107. The relevant body must also re-determine the salaries of all existing excellent teachers appointed on or before 31 August 2008 in accordance with sub-paragraphs 4 and 5.

108. The salary range for excellent teachers in inner London is £37,672 to £53,819 and elsewhere £37,672 to £48,437.

109. When determining the spot salary on the range for an excellent teacher, the relevant body must have regard only to the following:

a) the nature of the work to be undertaken; and

b) the degree of challenge to the role.

Review of salary

110. Excellent teachers are not subject to an annual review of salary. The relevant body may only re-determine the salary of an excellent teacher when there are any significant changes in:

a) the nature of the work to be undertaken; or

b) the degree of challenge of the role.

Safeguarding

111. Safeguarding arrangements now apply to excellent teachers' salary, should their salary be reduced as a result of the 1 September 2008 redetermination, or subsequent redetermination as a result of changes in the nature of the work, or the degree of challenge in the role. See paragraphs 21 - 24 above and www.teachernet.gov.uk/pay for further information.

Unqualified teachers (paragraph 37)

112. Schools should be aware that there are only three types of 'unqualified teacher' allowed by the law: trainees working towards QTS, overseas trained teachers who have not exceeded the four years they are allowed without having QTS, and instructors who are people with a particular skill who can be used for so long as a qualified teacher is not available. There is no other form of unqualified teacher permitted to teach in schools covered by the Document in England and Wales. All are paid on the unqualified teachers' scale.

113. From 1 September 2008, the unqualified teachers' scale is reduced from 10 points to six. Unqualified teachers who have previously worked as such must be assimilated from the previous 10-point to the six-point scale in accordance with the provisions of paragraphs 37.2-37.3. Unqualified teachers receive points on the previous pay scale before assimilation to the new pay scale in accordance with the assimilation table in paragraph 37.4. Such teachers receive a mandatory point for years of satisfactory employment since 1 September 2005, when points became permanent, and any discretionary points which may have been awarded. All unqualified teachers may receive points for other experience or excellence, and those working as unqualified teachers prior to 1 September 2005 and who have not worked as such since may receive a discretionary point for each year of employment as an unqualified teacher.

114. Those beginning work as unqualified teachers with effect from or after 1 September 2008 are placed on point 1 of the new pay scale, unless the relevant body determines that they have other relevant experience, in which case a discretionary point or points may be awarded.

115. Annex 4 covers arrangements for the award of points on the unqualified teachers' scale from 1 September 2009 onwards.

Unqualified teachers' allowance (paragraph 38)

116. The arrangements for paying an allowance to unqualified teachers have been modified with effect from 1 September 2008. Relevant bodies may pay an additional allowance to an unqualified teacher, in the context of their staffing structure and pay policy, if they consider that the unqualified teacher has

- a sustained additional responsibility which is focused on teaching and learning, and requires the exercise of a teacher's professional skills and judgement; or
- qualifications or experience which bring added value to the role he is undertaking.

117. The relevant body's pay policy should set out the way in which decisions are taken on allowances for unqualified teachers, so that there is transparency.

118. Where an unqualified teacher was in receipt of an unqualified teachers' allowance prior to 1 September 2008, the relevant body

must consider whether the allowance is in line with the above criteria, and if necessary, redetermine the allowance. If, in this instance, the new allowance awarded is lower, the difference will be safeguarded for up to three years.

119. Safeguarding arrangements now also apply to the unqualified teachers' allowance where reductions in the value of the allowance are made from 1 September 2008 onwards. See paragraphs 21 – 25 above and the safeguarding guidance at www.teachernet/gov.uk/pay for more information.

120. Unqualified teachers may not hold TLRs or SEN allowances.

121. Any scale points awarded to unqualified teachers are permanent, whether the teacher remains in the same post or takes up a new one.

122. Where an unqualified teacher becomes qualified the relevant body must redetermine salary and allowances in accordance with Part 2 of the document.

Social Priority Allowance (SPA) and Inner London Area supplement (ILAS) (paragraph 40)

123. Relevant bodies should be aware of the arrangements regarding teachers in receipt of the discontinued SPA and ILAS. All SPA and ILAS sums payable at 31 December 2005 are safeguarded on a cash basis for up to three years from 1 January 2006. All safeguarding under these provisions will therefore end by 31 December 2008. See paragraphs 21 – 24 above and www.teachernet.gov.uk/pay for further guidance.

124. If a teacher in receipt of SPA or ILAS safeguarding serves as a member of the leadership group, as an advanced skills teacher or as an excellent teacher in the temporary absence of the postholder, SPA and ILAS safeguarding is discontinued during this period but is restored at the end of the temporary period, unless it would otherwise have ceased under the provisions of paragraph 40.

Unattached teachers (paragraph 44)

125. LAs must take account of their pay policy and staffing structure when determining the remuneration of unattached teachers. LAs should therefore ensure that the pay policy and staffing structure are kept up to date in respect of their unattached teachers.

General safeguarding applicable to teachers taking up post on or before 31st December 2005 (paragraph 45)

126. Paragraph 45 applies to teachers who are subject to general safeguarding and started work in a new post before 1 January 2006. In addition to the longstanding provisions on the cessation of general safeguarding in paragraph 45.8 (including if the teacher refuses to accept an alternative post within the same authority), teachers' general safeguarding ceases if they move post voluntarily. In addition, should a teacher in receipt of a management allowance under general safeguarding accept a TLR which equals or exceeds the value of the management allowance, the safeguarded management allowance will end. If the value of the TLR is less than the value of the safeguarded management allowance, then only the difference between the sums will be safeguarded.

127. If a teacher in receipt of a management allowance safeguarded under general safeguarding is awarded a TLR in the temporary absence of the postholder, management allowance safeguarding is reduced or discontinued (as applicable) during this period but is restored at the end of the temporary period, unless it would otherwise have ceased under the provisions of paragraph 45.8.

General safeguarding applicable to teachers taking up post on or after 1st January 2006 (paragraph 46)

128. Separate safeguarding arrangements apply to teachers (including unattached teachers) whose general safeguarding started on or after 1 January 2006. Teachers in such cases receive as a cash sum the difference between their former salary and their new salary, safeguarded for up to three years from 1 January 2006. See paragraphs – 21 – 24 above and www.teachernet.gov.uk/pay for further guidance.

Safeguarding for members of the leadership group, advanced skills teachers and excellent teachers (paragraphs 47 and 48)

129. Relevant bodies should ensure that the mandatory safeguarding arrangements are applied to members of the leadership group, ASTs or excellent teachers who are subject to loss of salary as a result of

changes to the pay policy or staffing structure[13] (paragraph 48) (see www.teachernet.gov.uk/pay for further guidance).

130. If a teacher in receipt of safeguarding under paragraph 47 serves as a member of the leadership group, as an advanced skills teacher or as an excellent teacher in the temporary absence of the postholder, the safeguarding is discontinued during this period but is restored at the end of the temporary period, unless it would otherwise have ceased under the provisions of paragraph 47.

Relevant bodies should also note the need to redetermine the safeguarded pay of heads who were subject to loss of salary before 1 September 2005 (paragraph 48).

Part-time teachers Remuneration (paragraph 49)

131. All contractual arrangements entered into must comply with The Part Time Workers (Prevention of Less Favourable Treatment) Regulations 2000, The Part Time Workers (Prevention of Less Favourable Treatment) (Amendment) Regulations 2002, the Disability Discrimination Act 1995 (in particular the requirement for reasonable adjustments to be made taking account of the individual's specific needs) and the Sex Discrimination Act 1975.

132. Part-time teachers must be paid the percentage of the appropriate full-time equivalent salary as calculated in paragraph 135 below. The same percentage must be applied to any allowances awarded to a part-time teacher.

133. Part-time teachers cannot be required to work or attend non-pupil days, or parts of days, on days they do not normally work, but it should be open to the teacher to attend by mutual agreement with the head teacher (see paragraph 157 of this Guidance) and the pay calculation in paragraph 135 applied to any resultant additional hours worked. http://www.teachernet.gov.uk/management/payandperformance/pay/

134. The timetabled teaching week refers to school session hours that are timetabled for teaching, **including** PPA time and other non-contact time but **excluding** break times, registration and assemblies. The school's timetabled teaching week of a full-time classroom teacher is to be used as the basis for calculating the pro-rata percentage of the

13 For example, the relevant body should redetermine the pay range for an AST post where there is a significant change in the responsibilities of that AST, for example, if in-school subject leadership responsibilities are removed.

school's timetabled teaching week for which a part-time teacher is employed at the same school. This percentage is used to determine the pro-rata remuneration of a full-time equivalent teacher's remuneration to which a part-time teacher is entitled. The percentage remains the same whether the school operates a weekly, fortnightly or any other timetable cycle.

135. This calculation is specifically for establishing the proportion of remuneration (paragraph 49) **and** working time (paragraph 77) for part-time teachers and is to be used as the **benchmark** to determine a part-time teacher's pay and working time against the remuneration and working time of the teacher if he/she were employed in the same post on a full-time basis within the same establishment.

For example, if the school day, excluding registration and assembly, runs from 9.00am to 12.15pm and again from 1.15pm to 3.30pm with one 15 minute break in the morning session and one 15 minute break in the afternoon session the school's timetabled teaching week would be calculated as:-

	Morning Session (less breaks, registration, assembly)	+	Afternoon Session (less breaks, registration, assembly)	x	No of days in timetable (i.e. 5 or 10 days)	=	School's Timetabled teaching week (STTW)	% of STTW
Full-time	3 hours	+	2 hours	x	5 days	=	25 hours	100%

If a part-time teacher were employed for mornings only working 9.00am to 12.00pm every day their percentage of the timetabled teaching week would be calculated as:-

	Morning Session (less breaks, registration, assembly)	+	Afternoon Session (less breaks, registration, assembly)	x	No of days in timetable (i.e. 5 or 10 days)	=	School's Timetabled teaching week (STTW)	% of STTW
Full-time	3 hours	+	2 hours	x	5 days	=	25 hours	100%
Part-time	3 hours	+		x	5 days	=	15 hours	60%

In a case where the school day, excluding registration and assembly, runs from 9.00am to 12.00pm and again from 1.00pm to 3.30pm with one 15 minute break in the morning session and one 15 minute break in the afternoon session the school's timetabled teaching week would be calculated as:-

	Morning Session (less breaks, registration, assembly)	+	Afternoon Session (less breaks, registration, assembly)	x	No of days in timetable (i.e. 5 or 10 days)	=	School's Timetabled teaching week (STTW)	% of STTW
Full-time	2.75 hours	+	2.25 hours	x	5 days	=	25 hours	100%

If a part-time teacher were employed for mornings only working 9.00am to 12.00pm every day their percentage of the school's timetabled teaching week would be calculated as:-

	Morning Session (less breaks, registration, assembly)	+	Afternoon Session (less breaks, registration, assembly)	x	No of days in timetable (i.e. 5 or 10 days)	=	School's Timetabled teaching week (STTW)	% of STTW
Full-time	2.75 hours	+	2.25 hours	x	5 days	=	25 hours	100%
Part-time	2.75 hours	+		x	5 days	=	13.75 hours	55%

136. The relevant body should establish the proportion of the school's timetabled teaching week for each part-time teacher as a percentage of a full-time classroom teacher's school's timetabled teaching week using the same method of calculation as above.

137. Relevant bodies may wish to use the 'part-time teacher pay calculator' provided on TeacherNet. http://www.teachernet.gov.uk/management/payandperformance/pay/

Teachers working in more than one school or in a school with varying timetabled teaching weeks

138. The same calculations would be carried out by each individual relevant body or if a teacher works in different parts of a school with

differing school timetabled teaching week, two (or more) calculations would have to be made to arrive at a consolidated pro- rata remuneration for the teacher.

Unattached teachers

139. In the case of unattached part-time teachers the 'school's timetabled teaching week' comparator should be a full-time teacher within the same service at the Local Authority.

Leadership group/AST

140. The principle set out in paragraphs 132 and 136 above also applies to members of the leadership group and ASTs. Please also refer to paragraph 157 of this guidance about working time (pay document paragraph 77).

SECTION 3

Part-time Safeguarding (paragraph 49)

141. As a result of the new arrangements for calculating the remuneration of part-time teachers, while some existing part-time teachers may receive increased levels of remuneration, some may receive decreased levels of remuneration. Therefore safeguarding arrangements need to be applied, aligned to existing principles (see paragraph 47.7 of the Document). This applies to part-time teachers who were in post on 31 August 2008 and whose employment continues at the same school/in the same service from 1 September 2008.

142. So that part-time teachers who will be subject to safeguarding because of a change in the percentage of full-time remuneration they receive, will receive their 1 September uplift, the following sequence of calculations must take place with effect from 1 September 2008. The school should:

a. Calculate the salary that the teacher would have received on 1 September, had no changes to the part-time arrangements occurred, but without taking account of any progression ('the original salary').

b. Calculate the percentage of the school's timetabled teaching week applicable to the teacher (see paragraph 49.1.1).

c. Recalculate the teacher's salary on this basis, without taking account of any progression ('the new salary').

d. Calculate the safeguarded sum - the difference, if any, between the original salary and the new salary.

e. If the new salary is less than the total of the original salary plus the safeguarded sum, pay the safeguarded sum in addition.

f. Apply progression on the basis of the new salary, if applicable. If this salary exceeds the total of the original salary and the safeguarded sum, then safeguarding is lost. If it does not, then the safeguarded sum is paid in addition.

Allowances

143. Any allowances to which the teacher is entitled on a pro rata basis are increased if the teacher's remuneration percentage increases, but would not be decreased if the remuneration percentage decreases solely as a result of this re-calculation, until 31 August 2011 when safeguarding resulting from this change will end.

Teachers whose hours change on 1 September 2008

144. The 'original salary' in 142 a. above would be calculated as set out but using the new 'hours' percentage. After this, the remaining stages would apply as set out.

Existing safeguarding

145. Any existing safeguarded sums to which the teacher is entitled on a pro rata basis are increased if the teacher's remuneration percentage increases, but not decreased if the remuneration percentage decreases, as under normal arrangements that would in any event trigger safeguarding.

Additional payments (paragraph 52)

Continuing Professional Development

146. Relevant bodies should decide which CPD activities teachers may be paid for and set an appropriate level of payment in their pay policy. Heads and governing bodies should be aware that some teachers may not wish, or be able, to attend training courses in the evenings, at weekends or during holidays, and should respect the right of individuals to make their own choice, taking proper account of equal opportunities and contractual requirements for reasonable work-life balance. Payments to full-time classroom teachers should only be made in respect of those activities undertaken outside the 1,265 hours of directed time.

Initial Teacher Training Activities

147. Relevant bodies should decide whether to make additional payments to any teacher for activities related to providing initial teacher training (ITT). Such payments may be made only for ITT which is provided as an ordinary incident in the conduct of the school. Relevant bodies should set an appropriate level of payment for ITT activities in their pay policy.

148. Teachers undertaking school-based ITT activities do so on an entirely voluntary basis (*unless* they are ASTs for whom this is a professional duty). Such activities might include supervising and observing teaching practice; giving feedback to students on their performance and acting as professional mentors; running seminars or tutorials on aspects of the course; and formally assessing students' competence.

149. Other aspects of ITT activities cannot be regarded as an ordinary incident in the conduct of the school. Such activities include the additional requirements of School Centred ITT (SCITT), where schools take the lead in providing ITT courses. They may include planning and preparing materials for an ITT course, and taking responsibility for the well-being and tuition of ITT students.

150. Separate non-teaching contracts of employment should be issued to cover those aspects of involvement in ITT which require the exercise of a teacher's professional skills or judgment but which go beyond activities which may be described as an ordinary incident in the conduct of the school. No teacher should routinely carry out administrative and clerical ITT-related activities. Paragraphs 6 - 13 of Section 4 set out guidance on this, linking to paragraph 75.12.3 and Annex 3 of the Document.

Out-of-School Hours Learning Activities

151. Relevant bodies should decide whether to make payments to teachers who agree to participate in out-of-school hours learning. The level of payment should be covered by the school's pay policy. Payments to full-time classroom teachers should only be made in respect of those activities undertaken outside the 1,265 hours of directed time. All agreements and payments to be made should be documented. All such activities should require the exercise of the teacher's professional skills or judgment.

Recruitment and retention incentives and benefits (paragraph 53)

152. All payments for recruitment and retention purposes must be made under the recruitment and retention incentives and benefits provisions in paragraph 53. All teachers, including head teachers and other members of the leadership group, are eligible for such payments. Payments may be offered by relevant bodies and, where they are the teacher's employer, the LA. Payments under this paragraph may only be made for recruitment and retention purposes, not for carrying out specific responsibilities or to supplement pay for other reasons, and should be in line with the relevant body's pay policy. Relevant bodies/LAs are free to determine the value of any award. New awards may only be given for a fixed period of up to three years to new teachers for recruitment purposes, and up to three years for retention purposes. Awards made for retention purposes are renewable in exceptional circumstances. The relevant body or LA should determine the nature of those circumstances as appropriate and cover this in its pay policy.

153. All relevant bodies should consider as part of their pay policy deliberations (see paragraphs 11–13 above):

- whether recruitment and retention incentives and benefits should be offered to new or existing teachers; and
- if so, their nature, value, duration and the circumstances in which they will be paid.

154. Where a teacher is given an incentive or benefit under paragraph 53, written notification given at the time of the award should state:

- whether the award is for recruitment or retention;
- the nature of the award (cash sums, travel or housing costs etc.);
- when/how it will be paid (as applicable);
- unless it is a 'one-off' award, the start date and duration of the incentive (taking into account that the maximum of any one award is three years); and
- the basis for any uplifts which will be applied (as applicable).

Salary sacrifice arrangements (paragraph 55)

155. Employers may offer the salary sacrifice arrangements detailed in paragraph 55 to their employees if they choose to do so, and are encouraged to do so as the arrangements should be cost-neutral. Paragraph 55 permits teachers to participate voluntarily in such arrangements, subject to the limitations set out in the paragraph. Local authorities and governing bodies should ensure that any relevant information about such arrangements covered under paragraph 55 is passed on to teachers at their schools[14], to enable the teachers freely to decide whether or not salary sacrifice is an appropriate option. Participation in salary sacrifice is voluntary on the part of teachers. Employers may not make participation in a salary sacrifice arrangement a precondition for making an offer of employment to a prospective employee, or a precondition for promotion or some other advantage for an existing employee, nor may they withhold access from those wishing to participate.

Working time (paragraph 77)

Part-time teachers

156. The conditions of employment for part-time teachers mirror those of full-time teachers (see the Document Part 12). To avoid claims of discrimination against part-time teachers, schools should, as a minimum, ensure that their arrangements for the deployment of part-time teachers do not breach the relevant legal provisions regarding equal opportunities and unlawful discrimination (see paragraph 131 above).

157. The calculation in paragraph 135 is specifically for establishing the proportion of remuneration (paragraph 49) **and** working time (paragraph 77) for part-time teachers and is to be used as the **benchmark** to determine a part-time teacher's remuneration and working time against the remuneration and working time of the teacher if he/she were employed in the same post on a full-time basis. The calculation, which excludes break duty, registration and assemblies, does not mean that part-time teachers cannot be required to undertake such duties (see Part 12 of the Document). This does not determine the mix of teaching, PPA and non-contact time each part-time teacher does. So it will be possible for two part-time teachers at the same school to be on a 50% contract, but to each have different amounts of teaching time, PPA and non-contact time.

14 Please note that a form for teachers to register an interest in salary sacrifice with their employers, together with a note providing further guidance and links to sources of general information on salary sacrifice, is available on Teachernet at http://www.teachernet.gov.uk/pay.

158. The relevant body should establish the school's timetabled teaching week for each part-time teacher as a percentage of a full-time classroom teacher's school's timetabled teaching week using the same calculation as described in paragraph 135 of this guidance about part-time remuneration (Document paragraph 49).

159. Part-time teachers will have 'directed time' hours at this percentage of 1,265 hours; that being the amount that applies to a full-time teacher in any school year. Part-time teachers shall therefore be available to perform such duties specified by the head for their part-time percentage of 1,265 hours ('directed time') in any school year allocated reasonably on the days and sessions normally worked.

160. For example if a full-time teacher in a school has a timetabled teaching week (i.e. that school has a total school session time) of 25 hours and the part-time teacher's school's timetabled teaching week spans every morning from 9.00 to 12.15 (i.e. 3 hours excluding 15 minutes break) the percentage of part-time is 15 over 25, multiplied by 100 to produce 60%. The percentage is derived from the calculation for part-time teacher's remuneration, which is to be used as the **benchmark** to determine a part-time teacher's remuneration and working time against the remuneration and working time of the teacher if he/she were employed in the same post on a full time basis within the same establishment. Thus it would follow that the part-time teacher in the example would be required to be available for work for 759 hours directed time (1,265 x 60%).

161. Part-time teachers cannot be required to work or attend non-pupil days, or parts of days, on days they do not normally work. It should, however, be open to a teacher to attend non-pupil days or work on other days by mutual agreement with the head teacher. They may, however, subject to paragraph 162 below be required to undertake work that is within their allocation of directed time beyond that specified in the school's timetabled teaching week, allocated reasonably on any day or part of any day on which they are required to work.

162. The relevant body should ensure that, with effect from 1 September 2008, all teachers employed on a part-time basis are provided with a written agreed statement which sets out the expectations of the school, and the part-time teacher, regarding the deployment of working time. This should encapsulate both timetabled teaching time and leadership and management time where applicable. In addition the statement should also set out the expectations of the school in respect of directed time which is to be deployed beyond the school day.

163. The part-time teacher should not be subject to a greater proportion of their directed time to be allocated outside their normal sessions than are full-time teachers, as this may amount to discrimination. In arranging

meetings and other activities outside of school sessions, head teachers should try to minimise situations where part-time teachers are subject to directed time either side of a period when they are not required to be available for work on any given day by structuring timetables as far as possible to accommodate working patterns.

All teachers

164. The relevant body should ensure that, with effect from 1 September 2008, they consult with all staff on an annual calendar of staff meetings, parental consultations and other activities.

Leadership group/AST

165. Whilst, however, this principle is an appropriate mechanism for determining the salary of part-time members of the leadership group and ASTs, it cannot, as is the case with the directed time of classroom teachers, be used for the pro rata calculation of their working time. Members of the leadership group and ASTs do not operate on a time-bound contract and are not subject to the working time provisions of paragraph 77 of the STPCD, which define the working year as 1,265 hours allocated reasonably throughout the 195 days that constitute the school year. Nonetheless, the head teacher (or the relevant body in the case of the head teacher) remains duty bound to have regard to the work/life balance of such staff and should ensure that the workload of part-time members of the leadership group and ASTs is reasonable and that they are treated fairly in comparison with their full-time equivalents (see Document paragraph 56.4).

General

Relevant bodies should be aware of the requirements of;

The Working Time Regulations 1998 http://www.opsi.gov.uk/si/si1998/19981833.htm

The Part Time Worker (Prevention of Less Favourable Treatment) Regulations 2000 - http://www.opsi.gov.uk/si/si2000/20001551.htm;

The Sex Discrimination Acts 1975 and 1986;

The Flexible Working (Eligibility, Complaints and Remedies) Regulations 2002 http://www.opsi.gov.uk/si/si2002/20023236.htm

The ACAS Guide to Flexible Working -
http://www.acas.gov.uk/index.aspx?articleid=803

The Disability Discrimination Act 1995
http://www.opsi.gov.uk/acts/acts1995/ukpga_19950050_en_1

SECTION 4: Guidance on changes to the Document resulting from the National Agreement

1. This section of the guidance relates to the changes to the School Teachers' Pay and Conditions Document (the Document) arising from the National Agreement on Raising Standards and Tackling Workload (the National Agreement). It has been agreed and endorsed by the signatories to that Agreement, who believe that the changes are helping to reduce teacher workload and raise standards by freeing teachers to focus on teaching and learning. The signatories are committed to keeping the implementation of all aspects of the National Agreement under review.

2. This guidance refers to contractual changes to the Document that came into force in September 2003, September 2004 and September 2005. More detailed guidance is available at: www.tda.gov.uk/remodelling.aspx.

2003 CHANGES

ADMINISTRATIVE AND CLERICAL TASKS

Purpose of the provisions

3. Teachers need support so that they can focus on teaching and learning and expect administrative and clerical processing normally to be done by support staff and/or through more effective use of ICT. These provisions ensure that teachers cannot routinely be required to undertake administrative and clerical tasks.

4. The contractual changes apply to all teachers at a school, including teachers on the leadership spine and ASTs whether on permanent, fixed-term or temporary contracts and to teachers on part-time contracts.

5. The contract for headteachers never contained a duty to perform this type of task. However, some headteachers often felt obliged to undertake such work. That was a distraction from their leadership role. They should now have identified any tasks which are no longer necessary and delegated those which should be more appropriately carried out by members of the school support staff.

Defining administrative and clerical tasks

6. Some administrative tasks are straightforward – filing pupil records, recording absence data and collecting money. Others, such as administering examinations, ordering equipment and compiling and submitting bids require more expertise, but not necessarily that of a teacher.

7. Many activities in schools require a mixture of professional and administrative input. For example, writing reports on pupils' progress requires the expertise of a teacher. But that expertise is **not** required for many of the processes involved in producing the report - for example, "topping and tailing" reports or collating them either manually or using an ICT-based system. These elements should not routinely be done by teachers.

8. For the purposes of paragraph 75.12.3, the key tests for any task must be:

   a) Does it need to be done at all?

   b) Is the task of an administrative or clerical nature?

   c) Does it call for the exercise of a teacher's professional skills or judgment?

9. If the answers to a) and b) are yes but the answer to c) is no, then the task should not be carried out by a teacher. The list at Annex 3 in the Document contains a number of examples. It is not intended to be exhaustive.

"Routinely required"

10. Tasks do not have to be done on a daily basis to be classed as routine. Many tasks, such as collating reports, may only be done once per year - this would still be classed as routine.

11. Schools should ensure that their administrative systems provide appropriate support for teachers. It is important that teachers make good use of that support. This requires good organisation of administrative activities by all school staff – it would be unreasonable, for example, for a teacher to ask for large bulk photocopying jobs to be done immediately before a lesson. Schools must ensure that the administrative system in place is robust enough

to meet the continuing needs of the remodelling agenda, and that it is clearly understood by both those who use it and those who provide it.

12. The changes reflected in these legal provisions are not mechanistic or about narrow issues of job demarcation. They are about teacher time being more exclusively devoted to high quality professional teaching tasks.

13. Consequently, teachers should not be given the option to "choose" to do administrative and clerical work. It is not an appropriate use of teacher time. Head teachers should ensure that administrative and clerical tasks are not carried out by teachers, even where this involves a difficult adjustment for some teachers. Teachers' professional responsibilities are paramount and, in order to achieve the objective of raising standards and tackling workload, they must spend a larger proportion of their working time on those responsibilities.

Teachers with safeguarded management allowances for administrative and clerical tasks

14. There may be cases where teachers have safeguarded management allowances which were originally given for carrying out tasks that have been transferred to members of the school's support staff. In accordance with the safeguarding provisions at paragraph 5.1.2, the relevant body must review the teacher's assigned duties and allocate such additional duties as they consider appropriate and commensurate with the safeguarded sum, for as long as the teacher continues to be paid the safeguarded sum. In the context of the remodelling agenda any such additional duties should be focused on teaching and learning. There is no formal requirement to reach agreement on the nature of the additional duties, although it is good management practice to seek to do so.

15. Members of the leadership group whose previous responsibilities included tasks of an administrative and clerical nature that subsequently transferred to support staff should now be able to focus more on teaching and learning and to fulfil their contractual role, as defined in paragraph 65.2 in the Document. This includes: formulating the aims and objectives of the school; establishing the policies through which they should be achieved; managing staff and resources to that end; and monitoring progress towards their achievement.

16. Headteachers should ensure that these arrangements operate effectively.

Reviewing administrative systems

17. Administrative systems, and specifically the tasks listed in Annex 3, should be regularly reviewed to determine if there are different ways in which tasks can be carried out, or if they need to be carried out at all. No administrative task should be carried out by a teacher, which does not require their professional skills or judgement.

18. When giving administrative and clerical tasks to support staff, headteachers should have regard to the suitability of the task to the member of support staff's current role; whether sufficient time is available or could be freed up; whether additional training is needed; and any implications for pay and grading. Any revision of job descriptions should normally be agreed between the headteacher and the member of staff. Any extension of working hours must be by agreement.

19. Where the need for additional staff is identified, headteachers may wish to take the opportunity to consider whether the new post could embrace a number of the facets of extended support staff roles identified in the National Agreement. Many schools have also benefited from the creation of specific specialist roles such as health and safety officers, examination and timetabling officers, attendance clerks and technical support staff. Small schools may wish to consider whether, for certain tasks, a post (for example, a Bursar) could be shared with a neighbouring school or schools.

20. Experience suggests that support staff will become more efficient in undertaking administrative tasks than teachers, not just because of the better division of labour, but because for them these tasks will be a primary function, rather than an unwanted distraction from teaching and learning.

Management

21. Managing the work of other staff (paragraph 75.11) should not include routinely seeking or giving advice on contractual issues such as pay and conditions of employment. There is no requirement in the Document on teachers to provide such advice. These matters should be referred to the individual with specific responsibility for personnel issues and/or the employer.

22. Teachers have a duty to direct and supervise the work of support staff, including in particular those undertaking teaching and learning activities. However, it should not automatically follow that they are required to undertake formal aspects of their line management. Many schools see it as appropriate and good practice for this role to be undertaken by a more senior member of support staff.

WORK/LIFE BALANCE

Purpose of the provisions

23. All teachers and headteachers should enjoy a reasonable work/life balance. The Document has been amended to reflect this. In relation to headteachers, specific provisions have been put in place through regulations made under section 21 of the Education Act 2002 which put a responsibility on the relevant body (normally a school governing body or LA) to have regard to the work/life balance of the headteacher.

Implementing and monitoring work/life balance

24. Work/life balance is about helping teachers combine work with their personal interests outside work. It can help to recruit and retain better motivated staff through giving them greater control of their working lives and a stronger sense of ownership. A school that is committed to work/life balance:

- recognises that effective practices to promote work/life balance will benefit both teachers and pupils;
- highlights the joint responsibility to discuss workable solutions and encourages a partnership between individual teachers and their line managers;
- develops, monitors and evaluates appropriate policies and practical responses that meet the specific needs of the school, having regard to fairness and consistency; valuing teachers for their contribution to raising standards, not their working pattern;
- communicates its commitment to work/life balance to its staff;
- demonstrates leadership and encourages senior managers to lead by example.

25. Employers have a duty to employees at common law and a legal duty under health and safety legislation, including the Health and Safety at Work Act 1974 and related legislation and the Working Time Regulations 1998. In addition, four provisions have been put in place to encourage schools to develop effective work/life balance strategies:

- Additional hours for classroom teachers over and above the annual 1265 must be reasonable;

- For those teachers (deputy and assistant headteachers and ASTs) not covered by the 1265 annual limit on directed time, overall hours should be reasonable;

- Headteachers must have regard to the desirability of all teachers at the school (including themselves and other members of the leadership group) being able to achieve a satisfactory balance between the time required to discharge their professional duties and the time required to pursue their personal interests outside work;

- To the extent that headteachers direct their own work, they are covered by the provision above. However, specific provisions have been put in place through regulations made under section 21 of the Education Act 2002 which put a responsibility on the relevant body (be it the school governing body or LA) to have regard to the work/life balance of their headteacher and ensure that they are not required to work unreasonable hours and can achieve a reasonable work/life balance.

26. These changes form part of a wider commitment to secure downward pressure on excessive hours worked in schools over the four years from September 2003, with progressive year on year reductions from the current level of some 52 hours per week during term-time. Overall teacher hours will continue to be monitored by the Office for Manpower Economics on behalf of the School Teachers' Review Body on an annual basis.

27. Individual schools face varying degrees of challenge in achieving this objective. A number of other strategies support headteachers and governing bodies. These include:

- The revision of circulars 2/98 and 22/98 to deal with non-contractual provisions such as the conduct and frequency of meetings. These assist in tackling teacher workload and unnecessary bureaucracy at school level;

- The change management programmes in England and Wales, including advice and guidance from the Training and Development Agency for Schools (TDA) in England, as part of which schools are able to call on the support of a network of local facilitators/advisers;

- The operation of the Implementation Review Unit (in England) and the School Workload Advisory Panel (in Wales), which make a concerted attack on unnecessary paperwork and bureaucratic processes for teachers, headteachers and all who work in schools.

28. Effective preparation is essential in both introducing and monitoring work/life balance policies. Headteachers should consider how best to ensure that they monitor the work/life balance of their staff. Consultation with staff and trade union representatives could also aim to develop agreed strategies and procedures for monitoring. It is essential to communicate new or revised policies effectively, perhaps through non-contact days or the inclusion of work/life balance in staff reviews and appraisals.

29. Maintaining effective work/life balance requires ongoing monitoring and evaluation of work pressures. Some teachers may find it difficult to "let go" of work – in such cases headteachers will need to continue to take steps to ensure that such issues are addressed and resolved with the teachers concerned. It is not in the pupils' interest for teachers to be working excessively long hours.

LEADERSHIP AND MANAGEMENT TIME

Purpose of the provisions

30. Members of the leadership group need time to focus on their leadership responsibilities and be supported in leading the reform agenda and managing change in their schools.

31. Many teachers outside the leadership group also have some form of leadership and management responsibility, including those of subject leaders and co-ordinators, heads of departments or faculties, ASTs, special educational needs co-ordinators and initial teacher training mentors.

32. Teachers with leadership and management responsibilities are now entitled, as far as is reasonably practicable, to a reasonable allocation of time within school sessions([1]) to support the discharge of their responsibilities. This is in addition to the contractual provisions on work/life balance and guaranteed planning, preparation and assessment time (PPA), which was introduced on 1 September 2005.

33. The provision for leadership and management time applies to all teachers at the school with leadership and management responsibilities, whether employed on permanent, fixed-term or temporary contracts. It also applies to teachers on part-time contracts.

34. Head teachers are also legally entitled to a reasonable allocation of leadership and management time as a result of this and other amendments. These make it clear that leadership is one of the core duties of a headteacher and that they should be involved in teaching to such extent as may be appropriate having regard to his leadership and other functions and duties. In addition, provision for dedicated headship time was introduced on 1 September 2005.

SECTION 4

Implementation

35. Given the varying nature and extent of responsibilities held by teachers, it is difficult to identify a formula for the amount of time which might be appropriate for each responsibility. This is a matter for the school. Schools should keep allocations of leadership and management time under review.

36. The provision of leadership and management time is intended to be a contribution to the time needed to discharge the relevant responsibilities. Subject to that qualification, some time for leadership and management must be allocated within school sessions, taking account of the nature and extent of the

(1) The Education (School Day and School Year) (England) Regulations 1999 state that "every day on which a school meets shall be divided into two sessions which shall be separated by a break in the middle of the day" and that "at least 380 sessions shall be held at a school during any school year". Under SI 1999/2255 heads are required to inform parents of "the times at which each school session begins and ends on a school day".

responsibilities of each member of staff and the management structure of the school. In order for the time to be meaningful, it should not be allocated in short blocks, for example ten to twenty minutes here and there.

37. The Document requires cover to be allocated on an equitable basis. While leadership and management time may be used for cover within the contractual limits, it should not be used disproportionately.

38. Time for leadership and management can be identified using one, or a combination, of the following strategies:

- Existing non-contact time already allocated specifically for that purpose;

- Re-designation of some or all of any non-contact time previously allocated to support a variety of tasks, including those which do not require the professional expertise of a qualified teacher (and which should therefore be carried out by appropriate support staff);

- The release of teachers from pupil contact time which does not involve teaching. This includes pupil supervision, registration, attendance at assemblies and other similar tasks that can be carried out by appropriate support staff. Where appropriate, this should be in accordance with the provisions of the regulations and guidance made under section 133 of the Education Act 2002.

39. All schools should ensure that the allocation of leadership and management time is reasonable.

40. Schools should have ensured that whatever had already been done in relation to the provision of leadership and management time was sustainable in the context of PPA time.

No detriment

41. Where teachers already had timetabled non-contact time for leadership and management responsibilities, which was unaffected by the contractual change relating to administrative and clerical tasks, the amount of time should not have been reduced as a result of the implementation of the contractual changes relating to leadership and management time.

ASSIGNED TEACHERS

Purpose of the provisions

42. These changes were related to regulations made under section 133 of the Education Act 2002 and accompanying guidance. They were designed to protect the role of the qualified teacher and prevent job substitution. The provisions should be read in conjunction with the section 133 regulations and accompanying guidance.

43. The section 133 regulations clarify the respective roles of qualified teachers and other staff in schools, and specify circumstances under which certain kinds of staff without qualified teacher status (usually support staff) may carry out 'specified work' related to teaching and learning, including requirements for appropriate direction and supervision of support staff by a teacher.

44. The changes to the Document place a duty on headteachers to ensure that each class or group timetabled for core and foundation subjects and for religious education and each class or group in the foundation stage has a teacher assigned to teach it. The assigned teacher is responsible for the progress of the pupils in the class/group over the course of the academic year. Assigned teachers may be assisted in their work by other teachers deployed on the timetable to take that class/group for particular activities or lessons and/or by support staff, some of whom may carry out 'specified work'.

45. Paragraph 4 of Schedule 2 of the regulations concerns the appointment of instructors – person with special qualifications or experience or both. In circumstances where there is no qualified teacher, or trainee on the Graduate, Registered or Overseas-Trained Teacher Programmes available for an appointment, the body which normally appoints staff in the relevant school, either the LA or Governing Body, may appoint an instructor, provided that they have made the necessary judgement as to the instructor's qualifications and experience.

2004 CHANGES

COVER

Purpose of the provisions

46. Cover for absence is not an effective use of the time of teachers at a school. In the past, many teachers have borne a heavy burden of cover for absent colleagues, but this should be increasingly unusual. Downward pressure on cover should continue, to deliver the objective in the National Agreement that teachers at a school should only rarely cover for absent colleagues.

Definition of absence

47. Absence occurs when the teacher normally responsible for teaching a particular class is absent from the classroom during the time they have been timetabled to teach. The absence could be for a variety of reasons, including internal and external activities as well as sickness. It could be short-term or long-term. All absence needs to be carefully managed to minimise the impact on teaching and learning for the pupil.

48. On 1 September 2004, two contractual changes on cover came into effect:

- a limit on the amount of cover that can be provided by an individual teacher; and
- an amended duty for headteachers to ensure that cover for absent teachers is shared equitably among all teachers in the school (including the headteacher), taking account of their teaching and other duties, and of the desirability of not using a teacher at the school until all other reasonable means of providing cover have been exhausted.

49. The contractual changes apply to all teachers at a school, including teachers on the leadership spine and ASTs whether on permanent, fixed-term or temporary contracts and pro-rata to teachers on part-time contracts. A similar amendment to paragraph 60.4.4 also ensures that headteachers are covered by the contractual limit.

50. Schools should expect to implement the objective that teachers should only rarely cover from 1 September 2009. In the meantime, schools should set their own interim targets, informed by the latest OME data(2) which serves as a benchmark, to ensure they are ready to meet the objective of teachers rarely covering from 1 September 2009.

Reducing the burden of cover

51. From 1 September 2004, each individual teacher has had a 38-hour limit on the amount of cover he/she can be required to do in each academic year. This limit must not be exceeded. No weekly or termly limit within the 38 hours is identified within the contractual limit. However, headteachers should seek to ensure, as far as practicable, an even spread of cover throughout each term.

52. All cover for absence undertaken by teachers at a school counts towards the limit. The Document requires cover to be allocated on an equitable basis. Where schools designate on the timetable non-contact periods specifically for cover these must count towards the 38 hour limit on the occasions when they are used. Leadership and management time can also be used for cover but should not be used disproportionately. The time used counts against the limit.

53. The guaranteed PPA time of teachers at a school forms part of the legal conditions of employment and cannot be used for cover.

Gained time

54. During the academic year, particularly in the summer term, teachers who take examination classes/groups are often released from some of their timetabled teaching commitments as a result of pupils being on study or examination leave. Such time is known as gained time.

55. There are activities directly relevant to teaching and learning for which it would be appropriate and desirable to use gained time and

(2) OME data refers to the appropriate figures outlined in the most recent Teachers' Workloads Diary Survey published by the STRB, available at http://www.ome.uk.com/review.cfm?body=7.

which it would be reasonable for a headteacher to direct teachers to undertake. An agreed list of these activities is listed below:

- Developing/revising departmental/subject curriculum materials, schemes of work, lesson plans and policies in preparation for the new academic year. This may include identifying appropriate materials for use by supply staff and/or cover supervisors;
- Assisting colleagues in appropriate, planned team teaching activities;
- Taking groups of pupils to provide additional learning support;
- Supporting selected pupils with coursework;
- Undertaking planned activities with pupils transferring between year groups or from primary schools;
- Where the school has a policy for all staff to release them for CPD during school sessions, gained time may be used for such activities.

56. If teachers are directed to cover during gained time, it must count towards the 38-hour limit.

Educational visits

57. Educational visits are planned activities. Where teachers are absent due to participating in such activities, the absence is most appropriately covered by supply teachers or by using cover supervision. If a teacher at the school is used to cover for such an absence the amount of cover will count towards the limit.

58. Where a teacher acquires non-contact time in the timetable as a result of a class or group they would normally have taught being absent on an educational visit, then the guidance for gained time above should apply. Activities to be undertaken by teachers in such gained time must be planned well in advance of the visit.

59. The extended roles for support staff, which are an integral part of the remodelling agenda, provide the opportunity for schools to consider the use of appropriate adults, other than teachers, to undertake educational visits.

Exceptions

60. The only exceptions to the application of the contractual limit are teachers employed wholly or mainly to undertake cover.

No detriment

61. The amount of cover undertaken by teachers varies from school to school. There may also be minor variations for individual teachers from year to year.

62. Prior to the introduction of the contractual limit, in some schools teachers already did considerably less than 38 hours, while in others they did significantly more. Where the burden of cover was already less than 38 hours, no steps should be taken which would result in a worsening of the working conditions at the time.

Strategies for managing cover

63. Absence needs to be dealt with in a managed way to ensure that all possible steps are taken to enable pupils to continue to learn in spite of a teacher's absence. The strategies for managing cover need to take account of the type of absence. For example, long-term sickness, or maternity leave, will be more predictable and, therefore, more manageable than sudden illness. In order to protect pupil standards, longer-term absences should normally be covered by a qualified teacher.

64. Schools have a range of options for providing cover, including through supply teachers, higher level teaching assistants, cover supervisors, "floating teachers" employed for the purposes of cover, and, where other options have been exhausted, teachers employed at the school (within their contractual limit of 38 hours).

Supply teachers

65. Supply teachers can be used to cover for all types of absence. Where supply teachers are providing cover, they must, as far as reasonably possible, be actively teaching and not mainly supervising pupils.

66. It is also important that they are managed properly and effectively, with regard to their teaching and developmental needs. They should have appropriate access to CPD to maintain their standards of subject knowledge, pedagogy and behaviour management skills.

67. Schools are encouraged to adopt good practice in the use of supply teachers. This includes:

- careful induction into the school using materials that are matched to their period of employment;
- the provision of simply structured and clearly explained medium-term and short-term plans that also define the teaching expectations, the resources to be used, the demands that should be made of the class and the homework that should be set;
- the provision of information about the abilities and prior attainment of the pupils in the class;
- effective management so that all involved understand what is required and the professional standards that must be met.

These measures were identified in an OfSTED report on schools' use of temporary teachers (December 2002).

68. Schools also need to have regard to the Part-Time Workers' Regulations which in certain circumstances may apply to supply teachers. Those who are not casual (i.e. not employed on a day-to-day basis) have, under these regulations, an entitlement to pro-rata terms and conditions enjoyed by other teachers at the school. This would include access to CPD enjoyed by teachers at the school.

Cover supervision

69. Cover for short-term absences may be provided by persons who are not qualified teachers. To the extent that, during the period of cover, such persons are involved in specified work, they must operate subject to the regulations made under section 133 of the 2002 Education Act and accompanying guidance. Many schools have in the past employed such staff on a casual as required basis but now a permanent arrangement is likely to be more manageable and effective.

70. Those providing cover supervision may be existing members of staff whose job description has been reviewed in accordance with the first joint guidance note issued by the Workforce Agreement Monitoring Group (April 2003) or they may be new staff appointed on contracts which have a defined range of appropriate

administrative or support tasks, but which include cover as one of their key functions.

71. The headteacher needs to ensure that any persons used in this way have been appropriately trained, particularly in pupil behaviour management. Such training is essential if those responsible for cover supervision are to make a real contribution to reducing the burdens on teachers.

72. Cover supervision is particularly valid where work has been set, or where pupils are able to undertake effective self-directed learning, for example within an ICT Learning Centre in a school. Strategies should be devised to ensure that the arrangements for providing appropriate work for pupils who are being supervised do not place excessive additional burdens of planning, preparation and assessment on teachers. This could include developing banks of appropriate material and/or attaching a cover supervisor to a year band, department or faculty to enable them to, for example, support the teachers in administrative tasks and to be involved in the planning and preparation of cover when necessary.

Higher level teaching assistants

73. The primary function of higher level teaching assistants is to support and assist teachers. They may be deployed as one of the strategies schools choose to release teachers for guaranteed PPA time, provided that they carry out work specified in the regulations made under section 133 of the 2002 Education Act under the direction and supervision of a teacher.

74. In addition, they may be used for short-term cover, but headteachers would need to balance their use in this way against the educational desirability of regularly removing them from planned activities with the teachers to whom they are normally assigned.

Maintaining a record of cover

75. The member of the support staff administering the cover arrangements should keep a record of the amount of cover undertaken by each teacher. It is also advisable to maintain records of cover undertaken by other staff whose contract and job description specifies that a proportion of their time is/will be available to provide cover supervision.

2005 CHANGES

EXAM INVIGILATION

Purpose of the provisions

76. Invigilating examinations is not a productive use of teachers' time. From September 2005, teachers have no longer been routinely required to invigilate external examinations (e.g. National Curriculum tests, GCSE and AS/A2 examinations). Schools should have worked towards these changes and maximised the use of support staff as external examination invigilators, prior to the contractual change.

77. Teachers may, however, be required to conduct practical and oral examinations in their own subject area and to undertake the preparation of pupils and those aspects of assessment, recording and reporting associated with external examinations which require the professional input of a qualified teacher.

78. Teachers may also be required to invigilate internal examinations and tests where these take place during their normal timetabled teaching time. However, if a school reorganises the timetable for 'mock' examinations to replicate the external examination process then teachers should not be required to invigilate.

79. The principle underpinning the change is that invigilation does not require a teacher's professional expertise. In this context, it is a reasonable expectation that, subject to the agreement of the head of centre (usually the headteacher), a teacher should be present at the beginning of an external examination in their subject area to check the paper and to ensure that there are no problems with it. Those invigilating the examination should be made aware of the procedure for dealing with emergencies and for contacting a teacher in the subject area under examination should any candidate raise a concern or problem with the paper which requires their professional judgement. It may also be appropriate for a teacher to be present at the end of an external examination to ensure its efficient conclusion.

80. None of the tasks outlined in paragraph 79 above constitutes invigilation and all of them require a teacher's professional expertise. When carrying out such tasks, teachers should not be expected to stay in the examination hall/room for any longer than is necessary to perform them.

GUARANTEED PLANNING, PREPARATION AND ASSESSMENT TIME

Purpose of the provisions

81. The purpose of guaranteed planning, preparation and assessment (PPA) time is to relieve some of the existing workload pressures on teachers and to raise standards by providing some time for PPA within the timetabled teaching day.

82. Since 1 September 2005, all teachers at a school (including headteachers) with timetabled teaching commitments, whether employed on permanent, fixed-term, temporary or part-time contracts, have had a contractual entitlement to guaranteed PPA within the timetabled teaching day.

Principles underpinning the allocation and use of guaranteed PPA time

83. The amount of guaranteed PPA time should be set as at least 10% of a teacher's timetabled teaching time. Only teaching time within a teacher's 1265 contracted hours counts for these purposes, not other forms of pupil contact.

84. Guaranteed PPA time should be provided as part of a teacher's normal weekly or fortnightly timetable. It must take place, therefore, during the timetabled teaching day (i.e. during the time in which pupils are taught at the school) and must not be bolted on before or after pupil sessions. In order for the time to be put to meaningful use by the teacher, it must be allocated in blocks of no less than 30 minutes.

85. Guaranteed PPA time must be used for planning, preparation and assessment – these duties are contained in the relevant paragraphs of the Document. The time must not be encroached upon, including by any obligation to cover for absent colleagues. It is for the teacher to determine the particular PPA priorities for each block of guaranteed PPA time, although that does not preclude them from choosing to use some of the time to support collaborative activities.

No detriment

86. The 10% guaranteed PPA time is a minimum figure. Any teacher who was already in receipt of more than this amount of time specifically for PPA prior to the introduction of this change should not have had his/her existing allocation reduced to 10%.

Implementation

87. For teachers who did not previously have a regular timetabled allocation of non-contact time, a reduction in teaching time will have been necessary to provide guaranteed PPA time.

88. Other teachers may previously have received non-contact time, some or all of which may have been designated for PPA-related activities. Where additional time was needed to meet the minimum allocation for such teachers, then one, or a combination, of the following strategies may have been necessary:

- A reduction in teaching time;
- Changes in the use of existing non-contact time;
- Redesignation and redistribution of non-contact time currently allocated to teachers in the school for other tasks which will transfer to appropriate support staff, such as the administration of cover, organisation of work experience and the administration of examinations.

89. For example, a teacher who is timetabled to teach 20 hours out of a 25-hour teaching week must receive at least two hours of guaranteed PPA time. This time must appear on the teacher's timetable. Any non-contact time allocated for other activities (e.g. non-guaranteed PPA time, meetings, time for leadership and management responsibilities, and any time set aside to provide cover) must be additional to the guaranteed PPA time.

90. It should be noted that, in some cases, it is possible that teaching commitments will increase as a result of remodelling. For example, a teacher who previously had a reduced teaching load to enable them to carry out responsibilities that are now undertaken by support staff may have more time to teach once that transfer has taken place.

Use of higher level teaching assistants

91. Some schools may choose to use higher level teaching assistants (HLTAs) as one of the strategies for releasing teachers for guaranteed PPA time, providing that the headteacher is satisfied that the HLTA meets all the provisions of the regulations and guidance made under section 133 of the Education Act 2002. Where HLTAs are deployed in this way, the teacher's guaranteed PPA time must not be encroached upon. In case of problems with a class, the HLTA should use the school's usual referral system, in the same way a teacher would in case of difficulties or an emergency.

92. In some cases, HLTAs will be deployed to release teachers with whom they work regularly and where they are familiar with the programme of work of the class. This will help to maintain continuity and to enable the work of the HLTAs to be incorporated into the teachers' normal PPA cycle.

93. Other schools may deploy HLTAs in specialist roles where they have relevant expertise and/or training (for example, in sport or modern foreign languages), under the direction and supervision of a single teacher in the school. In either case, arrangements for deploying HLTAs should aim to reduce the overall workload burden on the teachers they support.

Newly qualified teachers

94. In addition to their guaranteed PPA time, newly qualified teachers also benefit from the contractual provisions of paragraph 60.9.5. This states that teachers serving induction periods under the induction regulations do not teach for more than 90% of the time a teacher at that school who does not receive payments in respect of additional duties or responsibilities would be expected to teach.

DEDICATED HEADSHIP TIME

Purpose of the provisions

95. Head teachers must have dedicated time to lead their schools, as well as manage them. Therefore, with effect from September 2005, governing bodies have needed to ensure that headteachers have dedicated headship time, having regard to resources in the school and to further national guidance that is being developed.

Context

96. Issues remain where headteachers with significant teaching loads (for example those who teach for more than 50% of the school timetable) have inadequate time during school sessions for their leadership and managerial role. The momentum behind the remodelling of the school workforce and a number of other specific provisions that have been introduced have helped here. These include:

- The work/life balance provisions;
- The introduction of leadership and management time and reference to the leadership function in paragraph 61 of the Document, which will effectively limit how much teaching a head can be expected to do;
- The limits on cover;
- Guaranteed PPA time, commensurate with their teaching load.

SECTION 4

SECTION 4